A CELEBRATION OF THE
DC3

A CELEBRATION OF THE
DC3

ARTHUR PEARCY

DEDICATION

Dedicated to Donald Wills Douglas, born Brooklyn, New York, 6 April 1892, died Palm Springs, California, 1 February, 1981. DWD was a design genius and his talent flowered with the Douglas DC-1 — the forerunner of the lesser known but equally successful Douglas DC-2 — and the most famous transport of them all, the Douglas DC-3. DWD was a great human being as well as a giant of aviation. He was the man who made commercial aviation possible through the Douglas Commercial series which revolutionised the airline business, and which included the DC-3.

First published 1985 by Airlife Publishing Ltd as *Fifty Glorious Years*

Copyright © Arthur Pearcy, 1985.

This edition published 1995 by
The Promotional Reprint Company Ltd,
exclusively for Bookmart Limited,
Desford Road, Enderby, Leicester
LE9 5AD, Chris Beckett Limited in
New Zealand, Reed Editions in Australia
and Booksales in New York.

ISBN 1 85648 245 6

Printed and bound in Hong Kong

Foreword

The period of 1932 to 1935, during which the Douglas DC-3 evolved from the DC-1 and DC-2, marked the transformation of Douglas Aircraft from fledgling status to maturity. This was a team effort but its success stemmed from the nature of Donald Douglas himself, whom we all knew as "Doug".

Doug set the tone, he established the rules, our decisions patterned his. The reputation of the company grew in harmony with his.

He knew the operation had to be profitable to stay alive, but he also knew that its products had to put technical excellence first.

As the company grew he had to withdraw from detail but he always kept in touch. His other love was yachtsmanship and sailing and he always put his hand on the tiller if we deviated from course.

Basically he was a superb engineer and designer and talked our language; He also learned to talk the language of lawyers, of businessmen, of financiers, and of the marketplace.

The result was that by 1936 our customers had such faith in our dependability and integrity that sometimes the order came first and the contract later, even in one case after delivery.

It was a lot of fun to work for Douglas in those days. The DC-3 was virtually unchallenged, for we had such a headstart that nobody else could catch up. We knew each other and our customers intimately. We were not overburdened by organization. But best of all, we were proud of our boss and felt that he was proud of us.

Arthur E. Raymond
Vice-President, Engineering, retired

Acknowledgements

The incomparable DC-3. All the words available in many languages have been used to exhaustion for 50 years to describe this unique aeroplane. The Grand Ole Lady started life with her nose in the air, and all those plaudits have not changed her attitude a bit. This is not a history of the DC-3, but a pictorial tribute in which I have attempted to portray those '50 Glorious Years' assisted by many personal friends, friends which the immortal DC-3 has introduced to my wife and myself over the many years of research into the type.

My first and most sincere thanks must go to the Douglas Aircraft Company and the many personnel who, over the past twenty years, have made us welcome at the Long Beach facility. Also for their encouragement and guidance with the books and other publications produced over the years on their product. Friend Harry Gann patiently allowed me into the Douglas archives on each visit in my search for the unknown photographs — we often found them. Austin J. Brown, The Aviation Picture Library, very kindly found me the photographs illustrating the front and rear of the jacket, and I feel sure that ex-DC-3 pilots will find that over the 50 years the cockpit layout has changed very little. The private photograph collections of many aviation buffs were placed at my disposal. These included, William T. Larkins, Gordon S. Williams, Peter M. Bowers, Peter R. Keating, Norman Taylor, Louis Vosloo, Roger Wright, Michael O'Leary. Martin Willing from Cathay Pacific submitted photographs of *Betsy* on her last flight from Australia back to Hong Kong. The South African Air Force kindly arranged for Louis Vosloo to fly a photographic sortie especially for this book. The parents of the late Stephen Piercy, Patsy and Ray, very kindly allowed me to use any of Stephen's large collection of DC-3 photos taken in all corners of the globe. Many of the major airlines and military air arms contributed photographs, as did the small operators, from cargo charter to tour operators.

Early in the book project we had an opportunity to visit and meet Arthur E. Raymond, design engineer on the early Douglas Commercials including the DC-3, at his home near Hollywood, California. We established a friendship which was sealed by our mutual admiration for the DC-3, plus a high respect for the genius who steered the ship — Donald Wills Douglas. My thanks to 'AER' for writing the Foreword to this tribute.

Sir Peter G. Masefield was a personal friend of the late Bill Littlewood of American Airlines, and Sir Peter kindly allowed me to use extracts from his mammoth paper *The First William Littlewood Memorial Lecture* which he delivered to the National Aviation Club in Washington, DC on Friday, 19 November, 1971. For this I am most grateful.

Lastly to Alastair Simpson, Director of Airlife Publishing Limited for his guidance, encouragement and personal interest in the subject and the production. My wife Audrey, who had I not had the good fortune to have served with the USAF on a C-47 'Gooney Bird' squadron I would not have met, has accompanied me on all my many trips far and wide in search of DC-3 information. She is now a fully-fledged member of the team. Even so, my grateful thanks for her continued patience and vigilance.

My sincere apologies and thanks to those I have not mentioned, but who contributed to this tribute to the Grand 'Ole Lady of the transport era, the immortal DC-3.

Fifty Glorious Years

Few, if any, of the many onlookers at Clover Field, Santa Monica, California, on 17th December 1935 could perceive the significance of the first historic flight of the Douglas DC-3 to commercial aviation. It was also the thirty-second anniversary of the Wright brothers' first flight. It revolutionised the concept of transportation and eventually touched the lives of people throughout the world. This new transport was an evolution of the earlier Douglas DC-1 and DC-2. It was twin-engined, had a gross weight of 24,000 lb and carried 21 passengers. The Douglas Aircraft Company constructed the transport in large quantities at factories located at Santa Monica and Long Beach in California, and Oklahoma City in Oklahoma. By the time production finally ceased in 1946, some 455 had been built as commercial models, and over 10,000 as military versions. No one knows how many are still flying, and one can only guess, but it is probable that the figure runs into hundreds commercially with additional hundreds in private service by corporations and individuals. A few years ago a private study by the author revealed that well over 50 air arms were equipped with the military version of the DC-3, many with no thought of a replacement.

Donald Wills Douglas, founder of the Douglas Aircraft Company, was born on 6 April, 1892, in Brooklyn, New York, the son of William E. Douglas, an assistant bank cashier. He witnessed Orville Wright put his box-kite biplane through its paces, and never forgot it. He later joined Glenn Martin in Cleveland, Ohio, and helped design a bomber before moving to the salubrious climate of California in March 1920 when he formed his own company. The Douglas Cloudster first flew on 24th February, 1921, the first aeroplane in history to airlift a useful load equal to its own weight.

Donald Wills Douglas, founder of the company bearing his name, headed a small team of engineers which included James H. 'Dutch' Kindelberger and Arthur E. Raymond, in developing the DC-3. The Grand 'Ole Lady was larger, faster and more luxurious than her predecessors — the airlines found her more economical to operate and safer. She was the first passenger airliner to be equipped with an automatic pilot, heated cabin and sound-proofing. Customer and passenger popularity for the DC-3 was based on these factors. Standardisation reduced maintenance and broke safety records.

William Littlewood, Vice-President, Engineering, of American Airlines, put forward ideas for a stretched wide-bodied version of the Douglas DC-2, which eventually became a completely new design, the ubiquitous DC-3. The first version was the Douglas Sleeper — DST — which was followed by the dayplane version. Costs per seat mile were about a third less than the DC-2. It was 64½ foot long and had a wing span of 95 feet.

Originally the DC-3 was conceived as a luxury sleeper airliner for American Airlines when it was found that the earlier DC-2 was not wide enough to accommodate a comfortable berth. Initial design was for seven upper and seven lower berths, with a private cabin in front. The engineers soon found that by removing the berths they could fit three rows of seven seats into the fuselage. Thus the DST sleeper evolved into the DC-3.

It was an immediate success when American Airlines introduced it into service in June 1936 on the non-stop New York to Chicago route. Orders from other airlines in the USA and overseas for more and more DC-3s came almost immediately. The airline industry converted to the DC-3 as fast as the Douglas factory at Santa Monica could produce them. By 1938 the transport was not only the standard equipment of the US major airlines, it was also operating in dozens of foreign countries. Travel coast to coast in the US was cut down to 15 hours. The President of American Airlines, C. R. Smith stated: 'The DC-3 freed the airlines from complete dependence upon government mail pay. It was the first airplane that could make money by just hauling passengers.' For all its unprecedented performance, the 110,000 dollar transport was not radically new technology, but rather a logical extension of the 14-passenger DC-2. The real break through was economy with the DC-3 becoming the standard airliner throughout the air transport world, confirming US manufacturing leadership and lifting American Airlines to a position amongst the leaders in the airline industry. There is always a turning point in the affairs of a company. That point for American Airlines, dramatically and decisively, was the introduction of the DC-3.

Any worries that the Douglas Aircraft Company may have had were over as the order book for the DC-3 filled up. In December 1937, just two years after the first DC-3 made its maiden flight, it was announced that the company had set an all time high in production. That month, alone, they had produced 36 aircraft and parts totalling 2,700,000 dollars with the new airliner making up the bulk of the orders. There was a backlog of 5,250,000 dollars in foreign orders for the DC-3, and 2 million more on the books for the US domestic airlines. By 1939 with the DC-3 in service all over the globe, the company employed 9,000 and the yearly payroll was 12 million dollars.

Credit .for the first ideas, and later more positive thinking, on the potential development of the DC-2 must surely go to American Airlines and its Vice-President, Engineering, William Littlewood; Discussions, as early as 1934, included C. R. Smith and centred around the possibility of a 'wide-body', longer-range, stretched DC-2 with more powerful 'G' series Wright Cyclone engines. As these discussions developed there were three obvious requirements. 1. Greater payload than the DC-2. 2. A body wide enough to accommodate berths on each side of the aisle so that the new transport could be used for trans-continental sleeper services, in succession to the Curtiss Condor. 3. Increased range to cut out stops between New York and Chicago and so achieve trans-continental services in four hops.

Design work started immediately under Arthur E. Raymond with basic layout under Ed Burton and aerodynamics headed by Dr. Bailey Oswald. They worked in close consultation with the National Advisory Committee for Aeronautics (NACA) — now NASA — plus personnel at the Californian Tech. Lee Atwood headed the stress department. On 10th May, 1935, Arthur Raymond produced "Douglas Aircraft Report No.1004" which outlined performance and weights of a DST (Douglas Sleeper Transport) development from the DC-2 to American Airlines' requirements. Douglas built a mock-up, expending some 15,000 man-hours on it.

Curtiss Wright had informed American Airlines of the possibility that the 750-hp R-1820-F engines of the DC-2 could, hopefully, develop into 1,000-hp R-1820-G engines by the end of 1935. Littlewood recalled that work started on the design of the DC-3 some 18 months before engines were available to power it. Initial ideas were that the new airliner would be about 85 per cent DC-2 and 15 per cent new with a 50 per cent increase in payload. In the end the DC-3 turned out to be almost wholly new with a wider and longer fuselage, larger wing span, more tail volume with a dorsal fin to stop the 'fish tailing' of the DC-2, a stronger undercarriage and more power.

But for the persistence of C. R. Smith there would have been no DC-3. Naturally Donald Douglas was reluctant to embark upon a new project at a time when he had a full order book for the DC-2. Smith made it clear that American Airlines would contemplate an order for up to 20 wide-body developments of the DC-2 if Douglas would build them. Half of the order being for 'Sleeper Transports' for 14 passengers, and the other ten as dayplanes with 50 per cent more payload and longer range than the DC-2. Reluctantly Donald Douglas agreed to go ahead with a design study, and Smith promised to send Bill Littlewood to Santa Monica to help.

Manufacture of the first DST began towards the end of 1934, with first engine ground runs taking place less than a year later on 14th December, 1935. Registered X14988 the first DST was at that time without the dorsal fin, later a characteristic of all DC-3s. It was added in March 1936 to improve stability on the approach. The engine is the heart of an aeroplane and no reference to the DC-3 should forget the two power plants which made it possible — first, the Wright Cyclone R-1820-G series of nine-cylinder radials and secondly the Pratt & Whitney Twin Wasp R-1830 series of 14-cylinder radials. They ranged in power from 1,000 hp in 1936 to 1,250 hp by 1939. Today many of the remaining DC-3s in service are powered by either Cyclones or Twin Wasps, with overhaul facilities and spares still available in many parts of the globe.

Carl A. Cover, Vice-President, Sales, and test pilot with the Douglas Aircraft Company, who first flew the Douglas DC-1, DC-2 and, the world-winner, the DC-3. Date of the first flight of the famous DC-1 was July 1, 1933, from Clover Field, Santa Monica, and was planned during the lunch hour for the Douglas employees. It is reported that Carl Cover was wearing a tweed suit and a bright green hat for this test flight.

The first flight of the Douglas DC-3 — the DST variant — was from Clover Field, Santa Monica at 1500 hours on Sunday, 17th December, 1935, with Carl Cover, Vice-President, Sales, as pilot, accompanied by two flight engineers; Ed Stineman and Frank Collbohm, plus Jack Grant, a mechanic. The flight lasted 30 minutes and was followed by two more to bring the total time that day to one hour 40 minutes. Everything went off smoothly. The date was a memorable one. Thirty-two years to the day after Orville Wright made the first heavier than air, man-carrying flight in a power-driven aeroplane at Kitty Hawk, North Carolina.

The transport was then flown daily from Clover Field — except for 21st December, Christmas Day, 27th and 30th December — right up to the end of the year. By 1430 hours on the last day of December a total of 25 hours 45 minutes had been accumulated, mostly by Elling H. Veblen, Douglas test pilot and M. Gould 'Dan' Beard, American Airlines engineering test pilot. For the first few days of January 1936 the new airliner was exhibited at the National Pacific Aircraft and Boat Show organised by Harry Wetzel in the Los Angeles Auditorium. Test flying was resumed on 6th January, chiefly by Dan Beard, with Tommy Tomlinson from TWA getting his first flight on that day. Between 11th January and the end of the month X14988 was grounded for modification to the propeller controls and exhausts. In spite of such interruptions, including a double engine change between 18th and 26th February, test flying of the DST went on more or less continuously throughout the first four months of 1936. There was no prototype. Most of the engineering test flying continued to be done by Dan Beard of American Airlines — an example of manufacturer and customer relationship which is perhaps unique, and it certainly helped to get the desired results. The second DST (NC16001) made its first flight on 4th June, 1936, a five-month interval since the maiden flight of the first DST, after which the transport was produced at an accelerating rate — 30 in the last six months of 1936.

The Douglas DST X14988 received its Certificate of Airworthiness — ATC 607 — on 29th April, 1936. The first batch of aircraft were certified at a gross weight of 24,000 lb. This was later raised to 25,000 lb and then to 25,200 lb as more engine power became available. After World War 2, DC-3s were certificated for airline operations at various gross weights up to 28,000 lb. On military operations C-47s flew regularly at 32,000 lb gross weight and more. Now registered NC14988 the DST was delivered to Phoenix, Arizona, and formerly accepted there by American Airlines. The airline had initiated acceptance in Phoenix for its DC-2s in order to avoid California sales tax, this being continued for all the DC-3s and other Douglas transports that followed. It was the DC-3 that swayed the balance sheet for American Airlines — in 1934 they lost 2,313 million dollars: in 1935 they lost 748,000 dollars, and in 1936, the first year of the DC-3, made its first profit of 4,590 dollars.

'Pat' Patterson, United Air Line's fiery and dynamic President who wanted a Douglas DC-3 that was different. He ordered the DC-3A powered by the 14-cylinder Pratt & Whitney Twin Wasp engines. The first DC-3A went into United Air Lines service on June 30, 1937, and made a profit for the airline.

August 2nd,
19 32

Douglas Aircraft Corporation,
Clover Field,
Santa Monica, California.

Attention: Mr. Donald Douglas

Dear Mr. Douglas:

Transcontinental & Western Air is interested
in purchasing ten or more trimotored transport planes.
I am attaching our general performance specifications,
covering this equipment and would appreciate your advising
whether your Company is interested in this manufacturing
job.

If so, approximately how long would it take
to turn out the first plane for service tests?

Very truly yours,

Jack Frye
Vice President
In Charge of Operations

JF/GS
Encl.

N.B. Please consider this information confidential and
return specifications if you are not interested.

SAVE TIME - USE THE AIR MAIL

TRANSCONTINENTAL & WESTERN AIR, INC.

General Performance Specifications
Transport Plane

1. Type: All metal trimotored monoplane preferred but
combination structure or biplane would be considered.
Main internal structure must be metal.

2. Power: Three engines of 500 to 550 h.p. (Wasps with 10-1
supercharger; 6-1 compression O.K.).

3. Weight: Gross (maximum) 14,200 lbs.

4. Weight allowance for radio and wing mail bins 350 lbs.

5. Weight allowance must also be made for complete instruments,
night flying equipment, fuel capacity for cruising range
of 1080 miles at 150 m.p.h., crew of two, at least 12 passengers with comfortable seats and ample room, and the usual
miscellaneous equipment carried on a passenger plane of this
type. Payload should be at least 2,300 lbs. with full equipment and fuel for maximum range.

6. Performance

Top speed sea level (minimum)	185 m.p.h.
Cruising speed sea level - 79 % top speed	146 m.p.h. plus
Landing speed not more than	65 m.p.h.
Rate of climb sea level (minimum)	1200 ft. p.m.
Service ceiling (minimum)	21000 ft.
Service ceiling any two engines	10000 ft.

This plane, fully loaded, must make satisfactory take-offs
under good control at any TWA airport on any combination of
two engines.

Kansas City, Missouri.
August 2nd, 1932

The saga of the Douglas Commercial began with a requirement formulated by TWA — Transcontinental & Western Air — in this correspondence which Mr. Donald W. Douglas Senior called 'The Birth Certificate of the Modern Airliner'. Considering the fact that one of TWA's major airports on its transcontinental route was Albuquerque, New Mexico, located at an elevation of 4,954 feet and with summer temperatures often exceeding 90 deg F, this requirement appeared, at the time, 'difficult' to meet. Arthur Raymond was rather concerned over the insistence that the new transport be capable of taking-off from any TWA airfield with one engine out. Then TWA's technical advisor, Charles Lindbergh, toughened the requirement still further: the new airliner now had not only to meet this demanding take-off performance, it had to be capable of climbing and maintaining level flight on a single engine, over the highest mountain along the TWA route. Raymond reported to Donald Douglas that he was 90 per cent sure that the DC-1 could meet the specified performance, adding, 'Its the other 10 per cent that's keeping me awake at night'.

During 1936 orders for the new DC-3 transport began to pour into Santa Monica. C. R. Smith wanted some of the 21-passenger DC-3s to augment American Airlines' fleet of DSTs. Jack Frye and officials from TWA started negotiations for a two million dollar order for a 23-passenger version of the DC-3. Eddie Rickenbacker followed suit to bolster the growing numbers of Eastern's 'Great Silver Fleet'. United Air Lines were also showing interest. The Boeing 247 airliner was the backbone of United, and there is no question that the low-wing high speed Boeing 10-passenger airliners were revolutionary. But the new Douglas Commercials out-performed them in every respect. As a result, in the Spring of 1936, W. A. Patterson, United's fiery and dynamic President, visited the Douglas factory with a blank cheque in his pocket to buy some DC-3s. United intended disposing of its Boeings in order to meet competition, and placed an order for 20 DC-3s. But the UAL aircraft would be powered by the 14-cylinder Pratt & Whitney Twin Wasp engines instead of Wright Cyclones. Because of this change the DC-3As, as they were designated, cost more. However they were approximately 14 mph faster, and the maximum altitude of 24,300 feet was ideal for United's routes over the highest peaks of the Rockies. Simultaneously with the announcement that they were buying DC-3s, Patterson announced plans for "Skylounge" flights, an extra fare introduced in a bid for the 'blue ribbon' New York to Chicago business. For an extra two dollars a ticket, passengers could have plenty of leg room and Club Car comfort. It was Patterson's answers to C. R. Smith's de luxe sleeper service.

The race was on for the trans-continental airline business. The first DC-3A for United went into service on 30 June, 1937, and it was not long before the airline had figures on the profit side of the ledger. The public liked the DC-3s luxury and her club-lounge atmosphere, including such innovations as electric razors, meals served on tables with silverware, real china and linen, plus air conditioning at terminals and aloft. United ordered more of the DC-3As and by December 1941 had a fleet of 39 plus 15 DSTs. Eastern acquired its first two DC-3s in 1936, and in 1937 retired five of its Lockheed Electras and bought eight new DC-3s. Traffic on the New York to Miami route was so great during 1938 that Eastern had to lease four DC-3As from United to use during the peak winter season. By 1941 a fleet of 36 Douglas transports were in regular use with Eastern. By 1938 the 50th aircraft had been delivered, and the DC-3 was carrying 95 per cent of all commercial air lines traffic in the USA alone, and was in service with 30 foreign air lines throughout the world. By 1939, 90 per cent of the world's airline business was being flown in DC-3s.

The one and only Douglas DC-1 seen on August 16, 1933, just six weeks after its maiden flight and prior to one of its many proving flights. At this stage it was in TWA livery, registered X223Y and was powered by two 710 hp Wright GR-1820-F3 Cyclone engines driving three-bladed Hamilton Standard propellers.

On Wednesday, July 1, 1935, the third anniversary of the Douglas DC-1's maiden flight, Donald Wills Douglas stood before the President of the United States, Franklin D. Roosevelt, to receive the Robert J. Collier Trophy, US aviation's highest award. The President read the citation: 'This airplane, by reason of its high speed, economy and quiet passenger comfort, has been generally adopted by transport lines throughout the United States. Its merits have been further recognised by its adoption abroad, and its influence on foreign design is already apparent'. This was just one of the many honours which the development of the DC-2 brought to designer and constructor Donald W. Douglas.

Under the leadership of its first managing director, Dr. Albert Plesman, Holland's KLM began to consider the impressive developments in air transport being made by the US west coast manufacturer Donald Douglas. This resulted in their combined entry with Douglas for the England to Australia air race, and as a direct sequel, their order for DC-2 and later DC-3 aircraft, this opening the way for a major invasion of Europe by Douglas. KLM set the pace in Europe, and in 1936, an initial order was placed for eleven DC-3s with thirteen more to follow. Thus the first European customer for the new DC-3 was Dr. Plesman, who by June 1937 had put it into operation along his Far Eastern route in place of the DC-2s. Only a short period of operation was required to demonstrate the great carrying power of the new transport, and soon KLM was handling so much mail that the Netherlands Government abolished the airmail surcharge. In addition to mail, Plesman's aircraft now carried eleven passengers, and there was a steward to look after them during the flight. By October 1937 traffic had grown to such an extent that he was able to run a service to Indonesia three times weekly. By 1938 KLM was planning its DC-3s as far as Sydney, and was talking about a daily service. From 1939 to 1945, virtually all services were suspended. Although Dr. Plesman died on 31st December, 1953, their link between KLM and the Douglas Aircraft Company was unbroken, and still remains unbroken today. It is vital link which in terms of both prestige and turnover must be of immense importance to both companies, and to world aviation in general, and it was undoubtedly forged in the race to Melbourne by the DC-2. Swissair and Air France were early operators of both the DC-2 and DC-3, plus ABA of Sweden, CLS of Czechoslovakia, Sabena in Belgium, LOT of Poland, and others. Douglas built the aircraft and Fokker in the Netherlands had the contract to build and assemble them.

With the advent of the DC-3, the airframe revolution was complete, and the modern airliner had arrived. Except for the introduction in the 1940s of pressurised cabins for high-altitude flights and tricycle landing gear that enabled aircraft to stand in a level position, rather than with their tails down, there would be no major changes in commercial aircraft design until the advent of the passenger jets some 20 years later. Even though it seemed just a scaled-up version of the DC-2, the Three, as pilots called it, was a significantly different and better transport. Its retractable landing gear was hydraulically operated, whereas it was manual on the DC-2s.

It was fitted with improved shock absorbers, and its adjustable propellers were of a more advanced design. Douglas engineers found that by enlarging the DC-3 fuselage there was a need to increase the wing span by ten feet, making the aircraft unstable. The wing had to be redesigned, and after exhaustive wind tunnel tests the Douglas design team came up with wings that were thinner than the DC-2s, particularly at the tips.

The result of these changes was hugely improved aerodynamics. The DC-3 was so easy to handle that it was said that the aircraft could almost fly by itself. Pilots quickly noted the difference. The DC-2 was known as a 'stiff legged brute' that was hard to land. Pilot-writer Ernest K. Gann, who flew both the DC-2 and the DC-3, described the latter as 'an amiable cow that was forgiving of the most clumsy pilot.' The added comfort and safety of the new transport was appreciated by air travellers, and by 1940 DC-3s had flown 100 million miles and had carried nearly three million passengers.

With just three Douglas DST airliners delivered, American Airlines launched its first non-stop Chicago to New York service on June 25, 1936, the first commercial operation with the aircraft which was to make history. The inaugural flight left Midway Airport, Chicago at noon CST on that Thursday morning, flown by Captain W. W. Braznell with First Officer W. A. Miller in NC16002 *Flagship Illinois*. The reciprocal service left Newark, New Jersey at 1330 hours EST the same day, flown by Captain Melvin D. Ator with First Officer F. R. Bailey in NC16001 *Flagship New York*. The group of American Airlines officials in the photograph include — l to r — M. D. Miller, T. J. Dunnion, Treasurer, Ralph Damon, Vice-President, and C. R. Smith, President who later became Chairman.

There is no doubt that the US Army Air Corps were envious of the new Douglas transports which were equipping the major airlines. Stress tests with a DC-2 showed that the Douglas design could be adapted for military use. Donald Douglas did not ignore the challenge put out by the Air Corps for a suitable transport, and in spite of a full workload with civil orders produced the Douglas C-33. Shown is a Douglas C-33 at the Rockwell Air Depot at Oakland, California in 1938, photographed by William T. Larkins.

The aircraft soon established a standard against which other airliners were measured. Its strength and resilience made it seem all but indestructible, and shortly after it arrived on the US airways system amazing stories — many of them true — began to accumulate about the DC-3. A Capital Airlines DC-3, involved in a mid-air collision with another aircraft, lost four feet from the end of one wing, including part of an aileron. Its pilot landed it safely in a nearby field with no trouble, and no harm to its full passenger complement. One DC-3 flying from Chicago to Detroit hit a down draught so severe that several seats were ripped from the floor, a number of seat belts snapped and passengers were tossed around in the cabin. After the pilot regained control of the aeroplane and landed, it was thoroughly inspected and found to have not one loose rivet or any other sign of damage. Another DC-3, on a flight from Atlanta, Georgia to Chicago, flew into a cold front and rapidly began accumulating ice on its wings and carburettor ice as well. The pilot cleared the carburettor ice by causing the engines to backfire repeatedly and endured updraughts and downdraughts which flung the aircraft from 5,000 feet to 13,000 feet and back down again. Eventually the pilot gained full control of the aircraft and made an emergency landing at Indianopolis after breaking the ice-caked windshield with a fire extinguisher so that he could have forward vision. Looking over the DC-3 on the ground, the crew found a two-inch layer of solid ice on the wings and tail that must have weighed over a ton. During the summer of 1941 a CNAC — China National Airways Corporation — DC3 had its starboard wing badly damaged in a Japanese strafing operation. The transport was fitted with the wing of a DC-2, the only one available, which, although five feet shorter, fitted and the airliner flew splendidly. This aircraft was christened the DC-2½.

Another fully documented tale of incredible DC-3 survival took place on 21 April, 1957, when the doughty transport lost 12-feet of its port wing to a mountain peak during a storm but flew on in almost routine manner, and made a safe landing at Phoenix, Arizona. There were 23 passengers on board this particular DC-3 which belonged to Frontier Airlines. Stories of the DC-3's durability are legend around the globe.

It is not generally known that towards the end of 1938 Douglas considered the development of a four-engined DC-3. Apparently in search of four-engine reliability, Panagra initiated interest in such an airliner for operation over their Caribbean and South American routes. On 17th January, 1939, Pratt & Whitney agreed to consign to Douglas by April four 9-cylinder Wasp S1H1-G engines with a take-off rating of 650 hp — 50 hp more than the standard engine — for use in a prototype aircraft. It was intended to replace the Stromberg NAY-9 float updraught carburettors with PD9-C pressure carburettors. Ultimately, an entirely new supercharger and rear section for the new engine was designed to employ Chandler-Evans carburettors. The four-engine DC-3 project was eventually shelved, and the Pratt & Whitney S1H6-G engine which would have powered production aeroplanes was not produced.

During 1935 the US Army Air Corps at Wright Field did static tests with a military DC-2, the aircraft finally breaking up under loads three times its design limitations. At this time the commercial DC-3 had a cargo version taking shape at Santa Monica and naturally the Army Air Corps were interested. US Government defence expenditure was centred on bombers, fighters and training types, leaving very little for transports.

Six Douglas DC-3 airliners, minus wings and tailplane spars, at Santa Monica on August 26, 1938. By the end of 1936, American Airlines had received seven DSTs and thirteen DC-3s, Fokker had received the first export aircraft, the Soviet Amtorg had taken delivery of one, and Eastern Air Lines had obtained two. United had received the first Twin Wasp-powered aircraft — five DC-3As and two DST-As. In July 1937 production of the DC-2 was completed. During 1937, 69 DC-3s were delivered to customers in the USA and 31 exported. The following year deliveries reached twelve in the US and 31 overseas. Fokker, who held construction rights in Europe, had accepted a total of 63 DC-3s and DC-3As. Production continued until the US entry into World War 2, the total DC-3 variants delivered amounting to 430 aircraft, with a further 149 ordered before World War 2 impressed into military use by the USAAF.

The DC-3 production line at Santa Monica on October 26, 1939, with 'Ship 227' 'Factory 2169' making its way towards completion to become NC21780 for Pennsylvania Central Airline delivered on November 29, 1939. By May 1959 it had logged a total of 53,338 hours and had served Capital Airlines and United Air Lines, was with Mercy Airlift in 1974, with World Gospel Crusade in 1977 and a year later was back with Mercy.

However Donald Douglas saw the specification issued by the Army Air Corps for a new type of cargo transport whose prime mission included the movement of supplies and personnel to front line airfields, and for the evacuation of sick and wounded. A payload of 3,000 lbs, top speed of 125 mph, and a range of 500 miles were included in the spec. Douglas saw in the DC-2 a transport that could be adapted to meet all military requirements so he submitted a formal proposal to build 20 modified DC-2s for the Army Air Corps at a cost of 61,775 dollars each, plus 20,500 dollars for the engines. Flight tests were held with the transport submitted, these including entries from Fokker, Ford, Bellanca and Fairchild.

The DC-2, modified to meet the demands of the Army Air Corps, was placed first with the aggregate figure of merit of 786 points. This resulted in an order for 18 Douglas transports, to be designated the C-33.

It is well worth recording that on the first day of June 1939, the 200th DC-3 — NC17340 *Oklahoma City* for American Airlines, was delivered.

By the time that the USA came into World War 2 in December 1941, a total of 507 DC-3s had been built of which 434 had gone to commercial airlines. At this time ten per cent of the transport aircraft in service with US airlines were impressed into military service. American, United, TWA and Western, volunteered to give up their DSTs because of the smaller disposable loads compared with the DC-3 — quoted as 8,250 lb against 9,155 lb. There were 50 DSTs built — 15 for American, 6 for Eastern, 17 for United, 10 for TWA and 2 for Western Air Lines. All of them were impressed into military service.

But the outbreak of World War 2, which was to interrupt the development of commercial air transport in Europe, resulted in a production programme for military versions of the DC-3, which was to establish the Douglas design as the greatest twin-engine transport the world has known. In addition to the 10,000 plus DC-3s built in the USA, it is estimated there were a further 2,000 plus built in Russia under licence as the Lisunov Li-2, and a further 500 odd in Japan — this latter transport being coded 'Tabby' by the Allies in the Pacific theatre and naturally often led to tragic recognition errors. By mid-1944 the Douglas Aircraft Company were turning out the military version of the DC-3 at the rate of one every thirty-four minutes, and by the end of World War 2 there were more of the type flying than any other aircraft in history.

In 1947 the US Civil Aeronautics Board — CAB — somberly considered the age of the DC-3, and her performance standards, announced that no more certificates of airworthiness would be issued. This grounding of the Grand 'Ole Lady was attempted on four occasions, but the outcry was such that the period was extended year by year until in 1953, it was announced that certificates would be obtainable for as long as the DC-3 continued to fly, even though it no longer fulfilled modern requirements. Records proved that the aircraft was still safe, still airworthy, and still able to do a job of work. One US airline, Lake Central, went as far as to study the possibility of putting the DC-3 back into production, with improvements, but was shocked to discover how much a new DC-3 would cost. During the 1950s, sporadic studies were made in Europe and the USA for what became known as a "DC-3 replacement". There were many contending designs put forward but the DC-3 remained in a class of its own in the world of 3,000-foot runways, at altitudes up to 8,000 feet and in temperatures up to 120°F — conditions which were all too common in the USA.

As one might expect, the history of the most versatile aircraft in combat would fill volumes, it participated in every theatre of action around the globe, flew the Atlantic and the Pacific, navigated the islands of the Pacific from the Aleutians to Australia, broke the blockade of the Burma Road over the 'Hump' route to China, towed the gliders which invaded and freed Europe from the Axis powers, dropped paratroops everywhere from Salerno to Corregidor, landed behind the Japanese lines with Orde Wingate in Burma, behind the German lines with partisans and agents in Europe, and earned itself many nicknames, amongst them 'Gooney Bird'. Apparently it was a name applied to early military models of the C-47, prior to World War 2, when there were no scientific methods of loading to ensure a proper weight and balance. Weighing of freight was haphazard, resulting in poor loading and overloads, which frequently could not be fully corrected in flight by trimming the aircraft.

In those days there were no concrete runways and operating off grass fields, sometimes soft due to rain or poor drainage, further complicated take-off. All these factors combined, resulted in attitudes of take-off and landing, not unlike the antics of the huge Pacific island sea-bird nicknamed "Gooney Bird". Who originated it for the C-47 will probably never be resolved, but it had to be one of those old pioneers, such as Verne Poupitch, Douglas test pilot of the period — who was one of them.

Production line at the new Douglas factory located at Long Beach during December 1942 with C-47 Skytrains being produced for the US Army Air Force. Records show that with few exceptions, the aircraft seen in this photograph were destined for the US 5th Air Force based in Australia. '118672' went to the US 10th Air Force in India and served with the India-China Wing of the huge Air Transport Command. The next two in line went to China. At this time the first R4D-1 transports for the US Navy appeared on the production line.

Not 1934, but 50 years later, 1984, the Anniversary Year of the London to Melbourne Air Race — the MacRobertson Trophy race when one of the few remaining DC-2s was shipped over from the USA to Holland in the livery of the KLM, DC-2 PH-AJU which came second in both the speed and handicap sections, and won the transport class event. This DC-2, seen flying over Amsterdam, flew the route flown by the 1934 DC-2 to Australia. On its return journey it suffered an engine problem and the Douglas Historical Foundation responded by flying out a spare engine.

It was the USAF C-47 and the RAF Dakota which originated the Berlin Airlift; a flight of C-47s which carried out the Arctic Ice Island exploration — the US Navy R4Ds which flew from the aircraft carrier *Philippine Sea* in support of Admiral Byrd's Antarctic research; the Greeks used ex-RAF Dakotas fitted with bombs when Communist guerillas threatened their recently won freedom. It was the C-47 which met the logistic problem in Korea during the early days of that war: it was the C-47 that fought with the French at Dien Bien Phu; she was recalled from storage for use as a gun-ship and interdictor in the controversial Vietnam conflict, and is today engaged in small brush wars in the outposts of the African and Central American continents.

Legion are the instances of flood, famine, pestilence, earthquake, volcanic eruption, tidal wave, hurricane disaster, to which the DC-3 has flown with humane results. Unfortunately she has been at the mercy of some of the world's extremist elements and used in gun running, drug hauling and illegal refugee carrying. No aircraft had been so historically abused as the DC-3, and yet come off so well. The 21-passenger capacity originally envisaged for the transport has been stretched many times. During the evacuation of Burma in World War 2, a DC-3 carried a total of 74 passengers, including Lt. Col. Jimmy Doolittle who was returning from his bombing raid over Tokyo. In Vietnam, many years later, a US chartered DC-3 carried well over 100 passengers from the northern plains to the safety of Saigon — it was admitted that many of the refugees were children who were strapped in two per seat, but it was never-the less another record for the Grand 'Ole Lady.

Just how long the DC-3 will continue to fly is anybody's guess. There are at least two still flying with well over 85,000 hours on the airframe. Second highest time aircraft is C-GDAK owned by the Canadian Warplane Heritage which is powered by Wright Cyclone 1,200 hp engines, has transported over a million passengers, flown 18 million miles, had 168 engine changes, and 1,000 tyre changes. Possibly the highest time DC-3 is a 1937-built transport now registered N136PB serving Provincetown Boston Airlines — the world's largest commuter airline today. The author flew in this aircraft from Naples, Florida to Miami International in December 1981 when its hours flown were breaking all records. Even by December 1978 it had a total hours flown of 82,873 and had flown 12,438,735 miles. Today PBA operates a fleet of no less than twelve DC-3s many of them flown by female pilots.

Worthy of record is the fate of NC14988, the first of over 10,000 to be built. On 14th March, 1942 with 17,166 hours 15 minutes in its log book she was taxied over from American Airlines hangars at La Guardia to the TWA hangars. TWA flew '988' in a stripped down configuration for 60 days on military air transport work within the USA. It was then turned over to the US Army Air Corps under the military designation C-49E and given the tail serial 42-43619. On 15 October, 1942, it was on a scheduled flight from its base at Knobnoster, Missouri, to Chicago. Two miles from its destination one engine cut. The aircraft crashed and burnt out killing all nine on board. Coincidental that the last DC-3 to be built, delivered to Sabena during mid-1946 from the Santa Monica factory, and registered OO-AWH, crashed at London (Heathrow) Airport on 2 March, 1948.

Today there are many museums of transport and aviation, who have been thoughtful enough to preserve the DC-3 within its walls or in its compound. Others are kept in flying condition. The Dutch Dakota Association in the Netherlands, who maintain and operate a DC-3, have long-term plans to preserve a DC-3 in moth balls, this to be brought out and flown on the 75th Anniversary on December 17, 2010, to show the children of tomorrow the plane that transformed air travel. If the time ever comes when it disappears from the skies it will be missed by the millions of friends it has made around the world. It was Donald Wills Douglas who said 'I do not believe that any of us who worked on the design and development, quite realised we were really building an airplane that would outlast the careers of us all. Perhaps she will fly on forever. I hope she does.'

Pioneer Days
1935 - 41

The first flight of the DST — Douglas Sleeper Transport — took place on December 17, 1935. By this time American Airlines had ordered ten DSTs and DC-3s, then doubled the order to eight DSTs and 12 DC-3s. Following initial test flying, the only modifications required was a dorsal fin-fillet to improve directional stability, added in March 1936, and some engine adjustments to restore full take-off power. On May 21, 1936, Approved Type Certificate — ATC 607 — was granted to the DST powered by 1,000 hp Wright GR-1820-G2 engines with an all-up weight of 24,000 lb. American Airline transports were all fitted with starboard side passenger doors to standardise apron operations with their earlier Ford Trimotors and other airlines followed this precedent. The dayplane DC-3 was given ATC 618 on August 27, 1936, followed by the DC-3A — ATC 619 — on November 28, 1936. The latter model was being ordered by United Airlines powered by the 1,000 hp Pratt & Whitney R-1830-SB3G engines.

On the other side of the Atlantic, in the Netherlands, Anthony Fokker built up an agency to include the DC-2 and DC-3 and eventually sold 63 of the latter to European airline customers. KLM was the first to place an order and operate the DC-3 in Europe. By the end of 1936 the order book for the new Douglas transport was beginning to fill up, and a total of 31 DSTs and DC-3s had been delivered, including twenty to American, seven for United, two for Eastern and one each for KLM and Russia. TWA — Trans Continental & Western Air — ordered the more powerful DC-3B, awarded ATC 635 on 3 May, 1937, powered by 1100 hp Wright GR-1820-G102 Cyclone engines with an all-up weight of 25,200 lb. This was a half-sleeper, half-day plane with eight bunks and nine seats, with roof windows over the berths above the third and fourth main windows.

Over the next five years a steady stream of orders flowed in to the Santa Monica factory, including orders from Pan American, Western, Australian National, Swissair, Sabena, ABA-Sweden, Air France, CLS from Czechoslovakia, Aer Lingus and LARES of Romania. These orders resulted from the remarkable economics of the new Douglas airliner. An increase of 3% in operating costs was offset by a 50% increase in capacity over the DC-2 allowing the airlines to make a profit without US government mail contracts, while at the same time providing a safe and reliable all-weather transport.

The first US Army Air Corps bulk order for the military version of the DC-3 was placed on September 16, 1940 involving 545 C-47 Skytrains, followed by a US Navy order for 30 R4D-1 transports. The type was eventually delivered in large numbers and in a variety of models developed for various military uses.

The first DC-3, a model DST-144 Douglas Sleeper Transport NC 14988 seen on June 24, 1936. It made its first flight on December 17, 1935 from Clover Field north of Los Angeles, taking off at 3pm and landing at 4.40pm. On March 14, 1942, '988' *Flagship Texas* of American Airlines with 17,166 hours and 15 minutes in its log-book, was taxied over from the American Airliners' hangars on the west side of La Guardia Airport, New York, to the TWA hangars on the east side. TWA flew '988' in a stripped down condition for 60 days on military transport work within the USA. It was then turned over to the US Army Air Force with military designation C-49E and numbered 42-43619. On October 15, 1942, while based at Knobmoster Field, Missouri, it was programmed on a scheduled flight to Chicago. Two miles from its destination one engine cut. The transport crashed and burnt and all nine on board perished. So ended, 6¼ years after the first flight, the career of the 'The First of the Many'.

Between 1935 and 1938, 50 DSTs and between 1936 and 1941, 381 DC-3 21-passenger airliners were built at Santa Monica. By the end of 1936 a total of 63 DC-3s had been sold which included 25 to American Airlines — 8 of them DSTs. Photograph shows a spectacular take-off shot of the fourth production DC-3, a DST model 144 *Flagship Massachusetts* which was delivered to American Airlines in June 1936. The Wright Cyclone R-1820-G5 engines developed 1,000 hp for take-off at 2200 rpm. This transport was impressed into wartime service as a C-49E between 1942 and 1944, was returned to American and later sold to Mexico.

Trans Continental & Western Air became the second operator of the new Douglas Sleeper Transport when it introduced sleeper equipment between New York and Los Angeles on June 1, 1937, and from New York to Chicago on June 18 with a 3 hours 55 minutes schedule. On August 15 TWA also added the 21-seat dayplane DC-3 during a period when it was benefiting from the award of new routes.

With the introduction of the DC-3, competition became intense and all airlines rushed to obtain fleets of the new transport from the Douglas Aircraft Company. It was not until May 17, 1950, that TWA changed its title to Trans World Airlines. In this photograph, a TWA DC-3 model 377C displays an advert for war bonds. This transport was built for American Airlines in July 1940 and was delivered to TWA on May 28, 1942. It was powered by Wright Cyclone engines and had a right hand passenger door. Unfortunately it crashed at Hanford, California on November 4, 1944, when a wing came off during a severe thunderstorm.

Superb night shot at Oakland Airport near San Francisco, a shiny new DC-3A-197C *Mainliner North Platte* of United Air Lines delivered on February 13, 1940. The rivet lines are visible plus details of the two Pratt & Whitney Twin Wasp engines and the undercarriage structure. By November 1956 this DC-3 had accumulated 47,919 flying hours having served with Southeast, Central and Frontier Airlines after United's use. During 1969 it was in use as crop sprayer in Tucson, Arizona and was last heard of with Air Indies Corp. in 1976.

A profile of the DC-3 can be obtained from this landing shot of a DC-3A of United Air Lines landing at Oakland Airport during 1940. It is *Mainliner San Francisco,* NC16063, built at Santa Monica in December 1936 and delivered to the airline a month later. The wing is so highly polished that there is a reflection of the undercarriage visible. This was the first Pratt & Whitney version of the DC-3 to be put in production. Twenty years later, in 1956 this transport went to Bonanza Airlines, and later to Edde Airlines, and up to a few years ago the aircraft was still in good flying order, and indeed may still be current.

United Air Lines, whose success with the new Boeing 247D airliner had been short-lived, now purchased 10 Douglas DSTs and 5 DC-3s, beginning service on the Los Angeles to San Francisco route on the first day of 1937. On the other side of the continent, the competition on the New York to Chicago route had become a battle. United Air Lines countered the growing threat of American Airlines with a luxury 'Sky Lounge' service, the DC-3 cabins being fitted with only fourteen swivel-seat chairs and the flights being made non-stop in less than four hours. This service commenced in February 1937, but was never an economic success and was discontinued in March 1939. This very rare photograph taken at Seattle, depicts a Boeing 247D NC13326 alongside a Douglas DC-3A-197 NC16070 *Mainliner Reno* completed at Santa Monica on November 25, 1936. Notice that both aircraft have right hand doors which is also unique.

United Air Lines preferred the Pratt & Whitney Twin Wasp powered version of the DC-3 which was designated DC-3A, the first being delivered in December 1936. The airline also operated a number of DST-A — Douglas Sleeper Transports of which one, *City of Seattle,* is photographed showing the Twin Wasp engines and three extra small windows towards the top of the fuselage indicating a DST model. This airliner, delivered on July 9, 1937, was impressed into military service as a C-48B between 1942 and 1944, before returning to United Air Lines. By the end of 1956 when it was in use by Southeast Airlines it had flown 48,361 hours. In 1968 it was owned by the Athletic Association of the University of Florida named *Fighting Gators* and is believed to be still in use.

Hawaiian Airlines was founded in 1929 by the local steamship company, when it was known as Inter-Island Airways. On the first day of October 1941, it assumed its present name and in the same year took delivery of its first three DC-3 transports, initiating them on inter-island freight services. This DC-3A N33608 *Princess Pewahi* was built at Santa Monica during August 1941, and converted to 'Viewmaster' configuration with large panoramic windows during 1955.

After the Russian state aircraft plant's leading aviation expert, Boris Lisunov, was sent to work at the Douglas factory at Santa Monica for two years to study the DC-3 production, a total of no less than 21 DC-3s were purchased for the USSR between November 1936 and March 1939. These aircraft were delivered by the company in the name of North Eastern and Excello, both represented by Amtorg, the Russian import agency. The first aircraft, registered NC14995 to Excello in November 30, 1936, was shipped to Cherbourg, France, the following day. This DC-3 was followed by a block of 11 delivered between May and August 1938, and concluded with a block of nine, the last of which was delivered in March 1939. This Douglas photograph taken in 1938 shows a Russian registered Cyclone powered DC-3 M132.

Towards the end of World War 2, during July 1944, American Airlines converted some of its DC-3 transports to cargo-liners. The *Flagship Airfreighter* pioneered cargo by air. NC 16002 was the third production DST, delivered in June 1936, and serving during World War 2 with the USAAF as a C-49E before conversion for cargo work. As early as 1940 United Air Lines had pioneered 'flying freight cars' with some of its Douglas DC-2 and DC-3 transports. Other airlines soon followed suit, flying mail in addition to general cargo. As can be seen in the photograph the airlines were used as flying billboards for the war effort, this one advertising War Bonds. On December 28, 1948, whilst owned by a transport company this DC-3 crashed in the sea on a flight from San Juan to Miami, Florida.

KLM Royal Dutch Airlines were the first in Europe to place an order with Anthony Fokker for eleven Douglas DC-3 airliners, with an option on a further thirteen aircraft. Of this pre-war order, one DC-3 PH-ARY was lost in an accident at Schiphol Airport, Amsterdam on November 14, 1938, whilst several others including a number of Douglas DC-2 transports were destroyed on the ground during an enemy air raid on Schiphol on May 10, 1940. The surviving DC-2 and DC-3 transports were flown to the United Kingdom and continued to operate with KLM in British markings. Shown here is the first DC-3 in Europe, assembled by Fokker, PH-ALI *Ibis* delivered on September 21, 1936, which fled to the UK. Unfortunately as G-AGBB it was shot down by a Ju.88 night fighter during daylight on June 1, 1943, over the Bay of Biscay with a loss of 17 lives including the film actor Leslie Howard.

The first Douglas Sleeper Transport — DST — was delivered on June 8, 1936, to American Airlines who introduced the type, as a dayplane, on the New York to Chicago route on June 25. The *American Eagle* and the *American Arrow* services, as they were called, set entirely new standards, with non-stop flights in both directions, thus surpassing TWA's DC-2 service of February 1935, which was non-stop on the eastbound flight only.

On August 18, American Airlines took delivery of its first DC-3, the production of which was now increasing. This released DST's for the job they were designed for, and on Sepember 18, 1936, the *American Mercury* inaugurated a skysleeper service from coast to coast on a 16 hour eastbound and 17¾ hour westbound schedule. At the end of 1936 American Airlines had in service 20 Douglas transports of which twelve were 21-passenger DC-3 dayplanes and eight 14-passenger DST's., the former used on the New York - Boston and New York - Chicago service, the latter on transcontinental services. Shown in this rare 1940 photograph is *Flagship Rochester* a model 277B DC-3, delivered in March 1940 with a right-hand passenger door.

Typical airport ramp shot anywhere in the USA during 1940. Luggage and freight is being loaded on the port side of this American Airlines DC-3 model 208-A *Flagship Phoenix,* delivered in February 1939. The passenger door was on the right-hand, or starboard, side of the transport and these were boarding when the photograph was taken. The three-wheel transport was typical of that period. This DC-3 served with American Airlines until October 1948 when it was sold to Colonial and then to Eastern Air Lines in June 1956. From January 1957 onwards it had a succession of owners, including the Roediger Bait & Fishing Hatchery in 1968. It was cancelled in March 1971.

The new World War 2 shadow factory at Long Beach, California, produced 4,285 C-47 military transports between 1941 and 1943 including this C-47B-1-DL 43-16299 seen on test flight over local terrain before acceptance by the US Army Air Force. The first two test flights were normally conducted by the company test pilots after which any discrepancies noted were rectified. After the second test flight the transport was signed off ready for hand-over to the military test pilots, who also usually made two flights, after which the Skytrain was made ready for formal delivery to the AAF acceptance team. After refuelling all loose equipment items were stowed on board along with a complete 'G' file of inspection forms, Tech. Orders plus weight and balance forms. Transports produced at Long Beach were taxied round the edge of the airfield to the Air Transport Command base at Long Beach Army Air Field, ready for their ultimate destination.

Glider-borne troop armadas, with Douglas C-47 Dakota tugs, were used in Europe, North Africa and in South East Asia during World War 2. The C-47 was capable of towing up to two fully laden gliders. On February 25, 1944, training for the Normandy landings began. By this time Troop Carrier Groups, of the US 9th Troop Carrier Command, were located at six bases on the western edge of East Anglia, five in Berkshire and Wiltshire, and three in Devon and Somerset. Two thousand gliders were assembled at Greenham Common in Berkshire during April and May 1944.

Training for the transports included troop flying, supply and medical evacuation missions within the UK. On D-Day, June 6, 1944, the combined US/RAF transport fleet was listed at 2,316 aircraft, the majority being Douglas C-47 and C-53 transports. This Douglas colour photograph shows a training flight of C-47 tugs and Waco gliders over unknown territory in the USA. Coincidental that the C-47 nearest the camera, 118385, built in 1942, is today preserved in Hong Kong and featured on page 96.

The US Army Air Corps were quick to recognise the potential of the new Douglas C-47 transport, and early models became involved in pre-World War 2 war games and manoeuvres in the field. This US Army Signal Corps photograph shows the fully armed field gun crew of seven complete with their Howitzer and jeep.

As the US Army Air Corps was already operating a number of military variants of the DC-2, it was natural for it to show considerable interest in the new DC-3, especially as its load carrying ability substantially exceeded that of the DC-2. However, funding limitations prevented the Air Corps from acquiring more than one military derivative of the DC-3, the Santa Monica built C-41A. This was ordered on August 17, 1939 and was delivered as a VIP command transport less than four weeks later. It was powered by two 1,200 hp Pratt & Whitney R-1830-21s, fitted with swivelling seats, and was essentially a DC-3A with military instruments and communications equipment. The VIP interior of the one and only C-41A is shown in this photography.

In service with The Great Silver Fleet of Eastern Air Lines since December 1936, the airline retired its last three remaining DC-3s on Saturday January 31, 1953. During that 17-year period Eastern's fleet of DC-3s — never at any one time totalling more than 63 aircraft — had accumulated more than 2,227,683 hours of actual flight time, giving a total off the ground time of more than 254 years. It is estimated the DC-3 fleet operated more than 83,584,318 miles.

World War 2
1941 - 45

As the 200th DC-3 came off the line in 1939 war clouds were looming in Europe, and wisely the development of a military variant was in hand. The first US Army Air Corps DC-3s were those commercial orders taken over on the production line. These received the designations C-48, C-49, C-50, C51, C-52 and C-68. At the time of Pearl Harbour in December 1941, a total of 289 DC-3s and DSTs were in US airline service, and in May 1942, 92 of these were impressed into military use becoming sub-types of earlier models, namely C-48B, C-49D, E, F, G, H and C-84. This included the very first DST NC14988 which became a C-49E.

For troop transport the C-53 Skytrooper was ordered in June 1941 with further contracts following for the C-53C and C-53D variants. In April 1941 a handful of impressed DC-3s went to the Royal Air Force serving in India with 31 Squadron, and in the Middle East with 267 Squadron. Most were flown out by Pan American Africa in US civil markings.

The Santa Monica factory, which produced all DC-2s and DC-3s could not cater for the C-47 production orders, so with government aid Douglas built a new factory at Long Beach adjacent to the municipal airport. A second factory was opened up in 1942 at Oklahoma City and produced the C-47-DK, C-117-DK and a few C-47C-DK amphibians. Under the huge Lend-Lease agreement hundreds of C-47s were delivered to Allies forces direct from the factories in the livery of the nation involved.

Those for the RAF were ferried via Montreal to Prestwick, or Nassau to the Middle East and India. The 700 C-47s for Russia were delivered via Fairbanks, Alaska by US ferry crews. By far the largest number, nearly 2,000, went to the RAF who adopted the name 'Dakota' for the transport, as did the RCAF, RAAF and RNZAF who operated the type. Some of the RAF Dakotas were diverted to South Africa, and a few are still in use today by the SAAF. Further Lend-Lease C-47s went to China, Brazil and France.

Many volumes would be required to describe the wartime activitives of the 'Gooney Bird' military transport which served with distinction in all theatres of operation. Suffice to mention that Douglas C-47 production for 1944 numbered no less than 4,853 transports, with 1,586 being produced between April and June. These included 1,237 USAAF Skytrains, 48 US Navy R4Ds, 218 RAF Dakotas, 7 RCAF, 8 RAAF, 4 SAAF, 2 RNZAF, 4 China, 3 Netherlands East Indies and 56 for Russia.

Braniff Airways was formed on November 3, 1930, and immediately prior to World War 2 was the sixth largest passenger carrier in the USA after the Big Four and Penn Central Airlines. Progressive improvements were made in equipment with Douglas DC-2s introduced during June 1937, followed by DC-3s in 1939. On August 15, 1952, Mid-Continent Airlines merged with Braniff. This model 314B Cyclone powered DC-3 was delivered to Braniff on June 20, 1941, to join a fleet of Super B Liners. During December 1959 it was sold to Southern Airways and converted to a DC-3A with the installation of Pratt & Whitney Twin Wasp engines.

Before World War 2 Delta Air Lines was quite small with a single route from Charleston, South Carolina to Dallas, Texas via Atlanta, Georgia and Birmingham, Alabama. By 1941, DC-3s had been introduced to be utilised on new routes — Knoxville and Cincinnati northwards and to Savannah, Georgia southwards. During 1943 New Orleans was added and in July 1945 a route to Miami with an extension northwards from Cincinnati to Chicago was authorised. This DC-3 model 357 *City of Atlanta* was delivered in November 1940 serving the airline until 1958 when it was sold to Mohawk and became N409D *Air Chief Mohican*.

Historic photograph taken at the Santa Monica factory on the first day of 1942 showing a variety of aircraft, many waiting for delivery to the war front. These include A-20 Bostons, C-47 Skytrains, C-53 Skytroopers. The Pan American DC-3 in the foreground is of great interest, being built for Eastern Air Lines in 1936, before serving with Pan Am and it is back at the factory for conversion as a C-49G for the USAAF. Whilst overseas it went to the Royal Air Force in April 1942, serving with both No. 117 and No. 31 Squadrons before being destroyed by the Japanese during an air attack on Myitkyina on May 6, 1942.

Early in 1942 in Australia, a unique organisation which was nothing more than a military operated airline was formed by the Allied Air Forces, Southwest Pacific Area, under the eventual name of the Directorate of Air Transport, or commonly referred to as DAT. It operated a diverse fleet of transport aircraft, flown by USAAF, RAAF, Australian civil and Dutch pilots, which were formed into transport squadrons. Many of the early transports used by DAT were Santa Monica built Douglas C-53 Skytroopers and this photograph shows a DAT C-53 landing at Three Mile Strip, New Guinea during 1942 with work still in progress on the runway.

Two Douglas C-47 Skytrain transports from a Southern Combat Air Transport unit with a top cover of Curtiss P-40 fighters, seen somewhere in the South-west Pacific theatre during 1942. *Sad Sack* is an early Long Beach built C-47 which was condemned in January 1943. The unarmed Douglas transports of SCAT ran regular schedules between New Zealand, Noumea, Efate, Espiritu Santo and Guadalcanal. As bases were built or airfields captured along the Solomon chain, the line was extended to SCAT. In a typical four weeks' operations report, one SCAT group logged 2,400 hours of combat flying in 948 flights, carried 1,320,848 lbs of freight, 543,629 lbs. of mail, 7,034 passengers and 198 medical evacuees.

Douglas C-47 Skytrain from the Jungle Skippers squadron of the 317th Troop Carrier Group drops a stick of paratroops onto the golf course at Corregidor on February 16, 1945. Many discarded parachute canopies from earlier drops litter the broken and cratered ground below. This remarkable photograph dramatically illustrates the difficulties under which the drop took place. For two days on the 16/17 February, the transports dropped the 502nd Parachute Regiment on Corregidor to open Manila Bay to US shipping.

For this operation the Group received a Distinguished Unit Citation for an operation performed at low altitude over small drop zones in a very heavily defended area. The Group was formed at Bowman Field, Kentucky on June 19, 1942, training with C-47s before moving to Australia at the end of the year and being assigned to the US Fifth Air Force. After the end of War War 2 it remained in the theatre as part of the Far East Air Forces being based in Japan at Tachikawa.

Of paramount importance to General MacArthur's and Admiral Nimitz's island-hopping campaign in the Pacific was the Gooney Bird's ability to fly in critical material that could not wait shipment by sea. A mixture of SCAT — Southern Combat Air Transport, comprised of US Marine, US Navy and USAAF Douglas C-47 Skytrains — is seen here at Pira Field, Bougainville, in support of strikes against the Japanese on Rabaul. SCAT was one of the inventions of Admiral Halsey, Commander Air South Pacific.

There wasn't a Marine at Guadalcanal who didn't credit the SCAT C-47s with saving the island more than once. Japanese dive bombers had blown up the tanker rushed in after the enemy had destroyed all the fuel dumps, meaning the USAAF fighter aircraft were grounded. SCAT came to their aid flying in 600 gallons of aviation fuel per C-47. It was a week before another tanker arrived.

The US 433rd Troop Carrier Group was activiated at Florence, South Carolina, on February 9, 1943 and with its recently delivered Douglas C-47 transports was trained to tow gliders and transport and drop supplies and paratroops. It moved to New Guinea via Hawaii, Fiji and Australia during August 1943 being assigned to the US 5th Air Force. It operated from Port Moresby, New Guinea and Biak until 1945 transporting troops and carrying such items as fuel, ammunition, medicine, rations, communications equipment and construction materials.

The Group with its six squadrons — 65th, 66th, 67th, 68th, 69th and 70th — moved to the Philippines in January 1945 assisting Filipino guerillas, evacuating prisoners of war and civilian internees plus transporting combat units from New Guinea, the Netherland East Indies and the Solomons to the Philippines.

From June to August 1945 it transported organisations from the 5th AF to Okinawa and carried occupation forces to Japan after VJ-Day. The Group moved to Tachikawa, Japan, on January 15, 1946. It was awarded a Philippine Presidential Unit Citation. Photograph shows C-47s from the 433rd Group unloading supplies for a fighter group at Finchhafen strip, New Guinea during 1943. The strip is made from PSP — Pierced Steel Planking.

As air transport increased, bringing supplies to forward units, the US Fifth Air Force started training teams, called Air Freight Forwarding Units. They set up an old wingless Douglas C-47 transport at the end of the landing strip at Seven Mile and practiced the art of loading and unloading. The time studies quickly showed the result. At first it took forty-five minutes to load a jeep and about the same to unload it from the Douglas transport. After a few days the time was down to two and half minutes to load and two minutes to unload. The trucks bringing supplies from warehouses to the waiting transports were loaded in reverse so that the cargo fed automatically and balanced correctly. Before long the C-47s were landing, unloading, and taking off at the rate of thirty to thirty-five per hour.

Whilst flying 'The Hump' or supply dropping, the Skytrain and Dakota transports were always under threat from attack by Japanese fighters. This rare photograph shows Vickers 'K' machine guns manned by RAF Dakota crew members. The fuselage is littered with an assortment of vital supplies to be air dropped. The left-hand crew member has an 'Air Gunner' brevet and 'CANADA' on his shoulder, whilst the one on the right could be a Chindit.

A Japanese Kamikaze fighter pilot attacked this C-47 Skytrain from the 1st Troop Carrier Squadron in Burma, and when he failed to shoot it down, he tried to ram it, resulting in the damage shown in the photograph. This is a good example of the ruggedness of the Gooney Bird, and there are many cases of damaged transports making it safely back to base despite extensive battle damage.

A Dakota from No. 267 'Pegasus' Squadron RAF bogged down at its base at Catania, Sicily during 1943. 'Pick-up' operations behind the enemy lines were an integral part of the activities of No. 334 Wing, which operated mainly from Brindisi. The Dakotas carried agents in and out, flew long-range sorties fitted with eight overload tanks in the fuselage, giving an endurance of 19 hours. On one of three 'pick-up' operations successfully carried out by Dakotas from No. 267 Squadron, important equipment relating to the German V2 rocket was brought out of Poland. The Balkan Air Force assisted Marshal Tito and his resistance fighters, and the Russians were based at Bari, Italy, with 12 Lend-Lease Dakotas and assisted in supply-dropping missions.

The 221 Douglas C-53 Skytrooper transports were troop-carriers built at Santa Monica, California, and powered by Pratt & Whitney 1,200 hp R-1830-92 engines. They did not have the large cargo loading door, reinforced floor or astrodome of the C-47. They were fitted with 28 fixed seats and a towing cleat for use as glider tug. Taken on January 27, 1942, this interior cabin view, looking forward to the cockpit, shows the bucket type seats in the Skytrooper, which possibly gave birth to the name 'Ole Bucket Seats' just one of many nicknames given to the DC-3 Dakota transport.

In addition to cargo and passengers many Douglas Skytrain and Skytrooper transports often carried auxiliary fuel tanks in the cabin, as seen in this C-53 Skytrooper on January 3, 1942. The wooden plank mounted on the tanks enabled personnel to visit the boys room at the rear. Some of the SCAT — Southern Combat Air Transport — aircraft carried two extra tanks in the cabin, just aft of the cockpit bulkhead. Oval in section about six feet long they were supposedly bullet proof. Extra tanks were fitted for long ferry flights, including deliveries of the transport across the north and south Atlantic ferry routes.

Camouflaged Dakotas of 267 'Pegasus' Squadron surrounded by peasants and their primitive transport at Araxos landing strip in Greece during September 1944. This unit flew an average of 1,000 hours per month in support of the Greek and Balkan campaign. The battle, involving the Greek islands of Cos, Leros and Samos, provided the Douglas transports with further exciting action. They dropped paratroops, carried 1,226 Army and RAF personnel to the islands, and 807,000 lbs. of supplies, petrol and ammunition for the Spitfire detachment operating from the islands.

These transports, often laden entirely with petrol and explosives, had to penetrate the heart of the German Aegean defences in broad daylight. When the landing at Cos became unfit for use due to enemy bombing, the Dakota crews threw supplies out through the aircraft's cargo doors.

Carrying ammunition and other vital supplies to the battle front, and returning from the area with casualties for field hospitals was just one of the many wartime tasks of the Dakota. This photograph taken on December 22, 1943, shows casualties from the front line being embarked on to a Dakota to Pomigliano, Naples. The aircraft is an early Long Beach transport which retains the USAAF fin number, but carries the RAF fin flash and fuselage roundel. It flew to North Africa from the USA in early December 1942, was based at Oran, North Africa in June 1943, followed by the Allied advance into Italy. It survived World War 2 and returned to the US to be used as a post-war DC-3 transport in a more peaceful role.

The Douglas C-47 fuselage is of all metal, semi-monocoque construction, almost circular in section and built up of channel-section transverse frames, or formers, and extruded bulb angle stringers. The framework is covered with an Alclad skin of varying gauges and is riveted with snap rivets. There are six compartments in the fuselage, which are, from forward to aft, cockpit, port and starboard baggage compartments, radio operator's compartment, main compartment and lavatory. This photograph dated October 9, 1943, shows the cockpit through the open radio operator's door. This C-47 is fitted with stretchers for casualty evacuation.

A total of six Douglas R4D-6 transports were transferred from the US Navy to the post-war Japanese Maritime Self Defence Force, which was based at Kanoya naval air base, on the southernmost tip of Japan. Prior to World War 2 the Douglas DC-3 was ordered by Japan through two trading companies, who between them purchased 23 of the new Douglas aircraft. Unknown to the USA, the purchase was directed by the Imperial Japanese Navy, who also purchased the manufacturing rights.

Production of the Japanese, built 'Gooney Bird', including two assembled from Douglas built parts, totalled 487. The type, code name "Tabby" with the Allies, operated with Southern Phillippines Kokutai squadrons attached to the various air fleets responsible to the Combined Fleet and to the China Area and Southwest Area Fleets. Crews varied from three to five and either 21 passengers or 9,920 lb of freight could be carried. By the end of World War 2, many had been destroyed. One did survive and was reported to be operating with the French Air Force in Indochina in the 1950s.

On November 26, 1950, a number of C-47 Skytrains from Flight 13 of the Royal Hellenic Air Force, were seconded to the USAF 21st Troop Carrier Squadron, to assist with the conflict in South Korea. These transports included 92620 *Jupiter*, 92622 *Neptune* and 92630 *Mars*. The photograph is of 92620 at K-9 airstrip, Pusan, South Korea on November 18, 1951. Greece was eventually liberated in October 1944, but was followed by a civil war in which the Communists attempted to seize power by force. A number of aircraft were obtained from the Royal Air Force including a number of Dakota transports which were modified locally for carrying bombs on racks under the fuselage, as temporary bombers. Today the Hellenic Air Force is assigned to NATO's 6th Allied Tactical Air Force — ATAF and still operates a number of Douglas C-47 transports.

Initially, the Super DC-3 was designated YC-129 with the USAF, but in recognition of its C-47 origins it became the YC-47F with USAF serial 51-3817. The USAF tested the YC-47F but placed no production order. The transport was then turned over to the US Navy in 1951 and became the R4D-8X with Build No. 138659, which for some unknown reason was cancelled and it became a standard Douglas R4D-8 — later C-117D — Build No. 138820 which is still around today. After storage at Davis-Monthan AFB, it is now registered N117LR to Mr. L. Richards, Chico, California. Photograph shows 138820 in US Marine Corps livery when it was based at Yuma, Arizona. It was previously with the US Navy at China Lake in California.

After the end of World War 2, the US Navy Department retained many of the hundreds of Douglas R4D transports they had operated over the years during the conflict. These were later handed over to other Government Departments such as the Federal Aviation Agency and the US Forest Service. This gaily painted transport, N645, was built at Oklahoma City as a US Navy R4D-6 and in the 1960s was with the Bureau of Land Management based in Alaska, hence the colour scheme. High visibility markings were used by most aircraft operating in the frozen wastes of either the Arctic or Antarctica.

Douglas C-47 Skytrains from the 438th Troop Carrier Group, under Colonel John M. Donaldson, USAAF, seen lined up at RAF Greenham Common during the early days of the assault on Europe in June 1944. The first two transports are from the 89th Troop Carrier Squadron — both Long Beach built — *Lilly Bell II* coded 4U-D for Dog, and 4U-N for Nuts.

The 438th Troop Carrier Group, with its four squadrons — 87th, 88th, 89th and 90th — was activated at Baer Field, Indiana during June 1943, trained on C-47s before moving to the United Kingdom in February 1944 assigned to the Ninth US Air Force. It received a Distinguished Unit Citation for dropping paratroops in Normandy and for towing gliders with reinforcements during the invasion of France. It dropped paratroops during the airborne attack across the Rhine in March 1945 and after VE Day evacuated Allied prisoners of war before returning to the USA during August/September 1945.

The 434th Troop Carrier Group, 9th Troop Carrier Command, USAAF, with its four squadrons — 71st, 72nd, 73rd and 74th — arrived at RAF Aldermaston, Berkshire, on March 3, 1944 from the USA. Here the Group remained until moving to France to Mour-melon-le-Grand on February 12, 1945. Photographed at Aldermaston a few hours before D-Day June 6, 1944, Douglas C-47 Skytrains with their Airspeed Horsa gliders are seen assembled on the runway prior to take-off.

The Group participated in the airborne assault across the Rhine, dropping paratroops over the east bank on March 24, 1945, and had resupplied US troops at Bastogne in December 1944 in the effort to stop the German offensive in the Ardennes. The Group received a Distinguished Unit Citation — DUC — and the French Croix de Guerre with Palm for providing supplies to the US Third Army during its drive across France. The Group returned home to the USA during August 1945.

Not many days after dropping paratroops over Normandy, US Ninth Air Force Douglas C-47 Skytrains of the Troop Carrier units were landing in France on roughly prepared strips such as the one shown in this photograph. Barrage balloons are in evidence. From strips such as this the many casualties were flown out to base hospitals in the United Kingdom. A number of USAAF C-47 transports were equipped with SCR-717 radar which had a tub antenna precluding the use of para-packs under the belly. These radar-equipped transports were used as lead aircraft for formations into battle and normally used by the squadron commanders.

The Douglas C-47 final assembly production line at Long Beach. The Skytrain was fitted onto carriers that ran on a rail and steel plate fitted to the factory floor. A dolly was placed under the tail wheel. Although the carriers ran straight, the aircraft was turned thirty degrees in relation to the final assembly line in order to conserve floor space. The particular batch in the photograph was designated C-47A-80-DL models. Many survived World War 2 and served with the post-war NATO air forces of Denmark, Norway and the Netherlands.

Douglas C-47 Skytrain transports from the 81st Troop Carrier Squadron, 436th Troop Carrier Group, seen on August 15, 1944, loaded with paratroops on their way to the invasion of Southern France from a temporary base in Italy. The Squadron dropped paratroops from the famed US 82nd Airborne Division over the Normandy beach head early on June 6, 1944. In July a detachment was sent to Italy to take part in the invasion of Southern France where it released gliders and dropped paratroops in the assault area. It flew several resupply missions to France and then returned to its base in the United Kingdom during late August. Both C-47 Skytrain transports in the photograph are Long Beach built aircraft.

Completed Long Beach built C-47 Skytrains lined up outside the factory awaiting delivery to the US Army Air Force. The C-47A model was an improved basic C-47 with a 24-volt electrical system. The C-47B was intended for use over the Hump to China with the gross weight increased to 30,000 lbs. and the two radial air-cooled engines centrifugally supercharged to obtain extra power. The C-47C was the amphibian. The model C-47D was an improved version of the C-47B except that the engines were not supercharged. During the month of May 1945, more than 415 C-47 Skytrains were delivered to the USAAF by Long Beach. In addition 120 Boeing B-17s per month were being produced.

On October 2, 1943, the Douglas Aircraft factory at Long Beach, California, completed the 2,000th C-47 built at that factory. It was a C-47A-50-DL42-24256 and Joe Messick, Public Relations Manager, wanted to make this roll-out a spectacular occasion. He had a double purpose in mind: it would be good publicity for the Douglas company and it would give a huge boost to employee morale and incentive.

When the transport was rolled off the production line, the Douglas PRO autographed the fuselage. By the end of the work shift, hundreds of production workers had done the same thing. Although the chalk was rubbed off before the Army Air Force would accept the transport, many 'Rosie Riveters' managed to get their names and addresses into the wheel wells and hidden compartments and thus started pen romances with the Air Corps mechanics who found them later.

Many military C-47s survived World War 2 and are still flying today. This early C-47, 41-7732 named *Miscellaneous,* a veteran of the South-West Pacific conflict, returns to the Douglas factory at Santa Monica where it was built in February 1942. It carries the US 5th Air Force insignia on the fin and a record of its supply drops in symbols on the fuselage aft of the cockpit. Douglas Boston attack-bombers can be seen parked in the background. This early C-47 flew to Australia on April 14, 1942, and after combat duty returned safely to the USA in August 1944 and was based at McClellan Air Force Base in California before being sold on the civil market in May 1945 as N68307.

The US ferry route to Russia was known as ALSIB — Alaska Siberia. This World War 2 Northwest Air Route stretched out some 2,210 miles from Great Falls, Montana, to Anchorage in Alaska. The apparent strategic importance of Alaska in the very early days of the war made this route seem vital to national defence as a means of reinforcing rapidly the meagre US forces there. After the Japanese feint in that direction in 1942 the danger subsided until Alaska ceased to figure as an active theatre.

From September 1942 to VJ-Day the chief function of the airway was the delivery of Lend-Lease aircraft to Russia via Siberia. This was as difficult as other tasks involving Russian co-operation, but it was a mission of great scope and importance, resulting all told in the transfer at Fairbanks, Alaska of more than 7,800 aircraft including over 700 Douglas C-47 transports. The photograph shows a Oklahoma City factory-fresh C-47 awaiting a ferry crew from the USSR to take delivery from Fairbanks, Alaska.

Early model of the Douglas R4D transport from VR-4 Squadron Naval Air Transport Service, seen over the rugged terrain of the Aleutians. Navigation aids were few and far between and the weather was not always as clear as the photograph tends to illustrate. Snow remained on the high peaks throughout the year. The Alaska-Aleutians flying operations provided a challenge that put the aircraft to supreme tests.

The extreme sub-zero weather conditions and the salt air atmosphere played strange tricks with engines, tyres, airframe and metal skin, hydraulic lines, brakes and other mechanical features. Oil became as thick as molasses, rubber fittings crystalised, grease froze in wheel bearings and the wind shields iced-up and frosted over. Crews learned how to winterize the rugged transports for adapation to the sometimes 40 to 50 degrees below zero temperatures. The Douglas transport came through with flying colours.

The USAAF Air Transport Command's Northwest route extended for a distance of 2,210 statute miles from the domestic terminus at Great Falls, Montana, to Anchorage, Alaska. Great Falls itself was remote from the centres of aircraft production located in California and along the Atlantic seaboard. Between Great Falls and Anchorage, the route's major bases were at Edmonton in Alberta, Whitehorse in Yukon Territory; and Fairbanks in Alaska. The latter two bases plus others used on the route were set in the midst of a vast wilderness whose surface, heavily wooded, provided relatively few recognisable landmarks for the pilot. Even in summer a forced landing was hazardous. This wartime photograph shows eight Douglas C-47 Skytrain transports flying over typical northwest territory, mostly uninhabited forestry and lakes. This squadron was based in Alaska.

US Army development of troop carrying gliders began in 1941, resulting in trials of the XCG-4A in 1942, this being a design of the Waco Aircraft Company, Troy, Ohio. Named the Hadrian by the Allies, the production CG-4 became the first and most-widely used US troop glider of World War 2. 16 different companies and assembly lines produced a total of 12,393. The CG-4A went into operation, rather disastrously, in the Allied invasion of Sicily in July 1943. Greater success attended their participation, in March 1944, in 'Operation Thursday', the second Wingate Chindit operation in Burma.

Subsequently this glider participated in all major airborne operations of which the most significant were the D-Day landings in France, June 1944; the landings in Southern France in August, 1944, the action at Arnhem and the crossing of the Rhine. Tugs were mainly the Douglas C-47 transport. This unusual photograph shows the first production Waco CG-15A glider, an improved model of the earlier CG-4A, which saw limited service in the last few months of World War 2. The configuration in the photograph was used to test highly technical communication equipment. The tug is a Long Beach built C-47A-35-DL 42-23918 which served with the 10th Air Force in India and later went to the United Nations as UNO-220.

A ferry flight of an unusual nature was that involving a Waco CG-4A Hadrian glider, which, fully laden with vaccine for the USSR, plus urgent radio, aircraft and motor parts, was towed across the Atlantic by a Dakota Mk I FD900 of RAF Transport Command during June 1943. The flight from Dorval, Montreal, to Prestwick, Scotland, was done as an experimental flight, the first of its kind and no special emphasis was laid on the accomplishment.

It provided information regarding the possibilities of an Atlantic air train service. Captain of the glider was Squadron Leader R. G. Seys of the RAF with an RCAF co-pilot, Squadron Leader P. M. Gobeil. The Dakota tug was captained by F/Lt. W. S. Longhurst, a Canadian with a New Zealander, F/Lt. C. W. H. Thomson as co-pilot. Departure from Dorval, Canada was June 24, 1943, and precisely on ETA the glider and tug circled Prestwick for the landing, as seen in this photograph, on July 1, 1943.

Possibly the most unusual of the Douglas DC-3 derivatives was the XCG-17 experimental troop-transport glider which had the two engines removed and fairings fitted over the nacelles. This one and only conversion was a Long Beach built C-47 Skytrain 41-18496 and was successful. It had a flatter gliding angle — 14:1 — lower stalling speed and a higher tow speed than conventional cargo gliders of the time. Empty weight was reduced from the normal 17,865 lbs. to 11,000 lbs but the normal gross weight of 26,000 lbs. remained.

Internally the cabin was lengthened six feet forward to accommodate 40 troops, or a payload of 15,000 lbs. A Wright Field project, the glider experiment was given to engineers of the Glider Branch who operated an experimental base at Clinton County

Army Air Field, Wilmington, Ohio. First flight of the XCG-17 was made from Clinton during June 1944, with Major D. O. Dodd at the controls. 400 lbs. of lead shot was added to the nose to ensure the glider was not tail heavy. After the first few flights this ballast was not necessary.

It became the largest glider in the USA, carrying a payload of seven tons. It had a very low stalling speed of 35 mph, could be towed at 270 to 290 mph but unfortunately there was no longer a need for this combat glider. It was delivered to Davis Monthan for storage on August 25, 1946, and during 1949 with reclamation complete, the engines were returned to the empty nacelles. It was sold as N69030 and was last heard of 'hail and hearty' in Mexico as XC-OPS with Petroleros Mexicanos.

When the huge Laister-Kauffman 'Trojan Horse' XCG-10A 42-seater was ready for testing towards the end of 1943, two Douglas C-47 Skytrain transports were used to get the world's largest glider off the ground. Once at altitude the lead C-47 was cut loose leaving one C-47 to tow the giant. This glider had a retractable nose-wheel and clamshell rear loading doors. Two XCG-10A's were built and as can be seen by the photograph, the whale-like glider completely dwarfed the two towing C-47s.

The unique floatplane version of the Douglas C-47 was nicknamed 'Dumbo' — its pontoons were 41-feet long, contained a series of watertight bulkheads and could carry fuel. However the weight and drag caused by the Edo designed floats on the Douglas C-47C was a serious handicap to its performance, and during July/August 1943 JATO bottles were fitted at Wright Field during tests to improve take-off performance.

The prototype XC-47C was a Long Beach transport turned over to Edo for the installation of an amphibian kit, whilst production floatplanes came from the Oklahoma City factory. Tests of the prototype were conducted at Floyd Bennett Field, New York.

Only five Douglas C-47C floatplanes were built for use in the Pacific and Alaskan theatres of operations, to be used on air sea rescue duties. Each transport weighed approximately 34,162 lbs. fueled and was powered by two Pratt & Whitney R-1830-92 engines. The floatplanes were approximately 30 mph slower than the conventional C-47.

The Douglas Dakota entered regular service with the Royal Canadian Air Force on March 29, 1943, when the first C-47 transport was delivered to No. 12 Communication Squadron based at Rockcliffe. As World War 2 progressed, an ever-increasing number were taken on charge and more units formed.

Over 200 Dakotas were eventually used by the RCAF with two squadrons operating in South East Asia Command, and one squadron based in the United Kingdom which took part in the Arnhem 'Operation Market Garden' campaign, towing gliders and dropping supplies. The photograph shows Dakota Mk. III FL618 seen flying over the eastern Canadian seaboard during World War 2. It joined the RCAF in 1944, and after the War went to Trans Canada Airlines, later going to the USA to fly with Frontier Airlines.

The main World War 2 base for BOAC in the United Kingdom, up to November 1, 1944, when operations moved to Hurn, Bournemouth, was Whitchurch near Bristol. Subsidiary bases were at Croydon, Lyneham, Leuchars in Scotland, and, as the war progressed in the Allies' favour, Cairo, Egypt. When Dakota flights were made on behalf of RAF Transport Command, aircraft carried military markings and RAF serial numbers instead of civil registrations.

Most of the BOAC fleet changed guise many times, and even the crews had two sets of uniforms. This photograph of a wartime BOAC Dakota shows the ground crew loading ballast as the aircraft is being prepared for a flight to Whitchurch for overhaul. A Oklahoma City built C-47B Dakota Mk. III KJ811 civil registration G-AGKD, it survived the war, being passed on to British European Airways and it crashed at Malta on December 23, 1946.

'The R4D has again proven herself a valuable friend and the "Grand Old Lady" of Antarctic Operations. She is economical and durable, and her versatility in short range, open field ski operations remains undisputed. It is not difficult to foresee the day, perhaps in the near future, when an equally versatile longer-range, greater-payload, higher-flying turboprop replaces the old warrior, but until that day comes, treat her kindly, keep her warm, push the right JATO buttons, and navigate clear of all obstacles.' So wrote Commander M. D. Greenwell, US Navy, Commanding Officer of VX-6 Squadron during Operation Deep Freeze 62.

Although VX-6 was to continue to employ the R4D in the Antarctic until December 1967, Commander Greenwell's statement had something of a valedictory about it. Photographed on a landing-ground in the snow and ice of Antarctica is Douglas R4D-8 BuNo. 17188 JD/7 which arrived in time to participate in Operation Deep Freeze 58. On November 12, 1962, whilst landing a University of Michigan geological party in the Horlick Mountains, a pin sheared in the port landing gear. It was determined that damage was sufficient and the location was so remote as to make repairs unfeasible, and the aircraft was abandoned. The party it had carried, later returned to the area and, during a storm, took refuge for five days in the derelict fuselage, a use never intended by the manufacturer.

A survey of the US Army aircraft inventory status on January 31, 1972, revealed that there were currently no less than 30 Douglas C-47 transports in service in the USA and overseas. In the USA, the Douglas transport served with the 3rd, 5th and 6th US Army, the John F. Kennedy Center for Military Assistance at Fort Bragg, North Carolina, and the US Army Parachute Team *Golden Knights* based also at Fort Bragg.

One C-47, ex-US Navy 17276, serving with the US Army Flight Training Center at Fort Stewart, Georgia, had the original starboard engine still fitted. This was a Pratt & Whitney R-1830-90D Twin Wasp manufactured by the Buick Motor Division of General Motors in the early 1940s. The cylinders were original, never chromed, and were bored twenty-thousandth oversize. One US Army C-47 had SLAR — Sideways Looking Airborne Radar — fitted, and most were heavily modified with nav aids and airborne radar. This photograph shows a very new US Army C-47 68836 based at the Red River Army Depot, Texarkana, Texas. Note the air-stair door plus the steel planking parking area.

Carrying the distinctive camouflage used in the Vietnam conflict and the tail-code of 361st Tactical Electronic Warfare Squadron based at Phu Cat Air Force Base, South Vietnam, this Douglas EC-47P-30-DK 44-76668 was one of many of the type converted for use in South East Asia by the USAF. Later for use by the South Vietnamese Air Force plus Cambodian and Thailand Air Forces.

Filled with ECM — Electronic Counter-Measure — equipment, extras included VHF and UHF radio, a FM command radio for use between the aircraft and ground troops, plus the usual TACAN, Liaison and IFF equipment. Chaff dispensers were also carried. The crew normally consisted of an aircraft commander/pilot, co-pilot, navigator and three airmen who operated the electronic warfare gear, and also a South Vietnamese interpreter for communication with the ARVN troops. This photograph was taken over Laos on April 3, 1971.

When the first Douglas DC-10 was delivered after certification on July 29, 1971, at Long Beach, a DC-3, N999Z, in American Airlines livery was present and caused great interest as seen by the colourful photograph taken on the day. This DC-3, built originally for United Airlines in 1942, was impressed into military service as a C-53C and served in North Africa with the USAAF before returning to the US in 1945. In November 1945 it went to Braniff and to Southern Airways in December 1952, becoming N999Z in May 1967. After several private owners it was broken up in May 1978.

Post-War Years 1945 - 85

At the end of World War 2, with deliveries complete, Douglas built a number of DC-3Ds from surplus airframes, and rebuilt a number of C-47s as DC-3Cs. The flood of surplus wartime C-47s so affected the market that orders were not forthcoming. Huge storage depots for surplus transports were set up in Germany, Italy, Egypt, India and the Far East, whilst many were ferried to the USA for storage. Some C-47s were sold for salvage overseas, whilst many more were rebuilt and are still flying today.

In June 1948 a massive airlift was put into operation to keep the city of Berlin supplied during the Russian blockade. Nearly 100 USAF C-47s were mustered to commence this mission of mercy, supported by RAF Dakota squadrons reformed for the airlift. Douglas C-47s from USAF units in Japan were involved in the Korean conflict in June 1950, and continued to support the United Nations drive against the communists. The USAF assisted the French in Indo-China during 1953 with C-47 support and maintenance, and gave the same assistance to South Vietnam in 1955 after independence. Viet Cong activity increased and eventually the AC-47 Gunship went into action with great success, supported by such heavily modified variants as the EC-47N, P and Q, the latter equipped with sophisticated electronic gear. Some were refitted with R-2000 engines to cater for the extra power requirement. The Vietnam conflict was to see the swan song for the USAF C-47, but it has been involved in many bush wars since, and over 50 military air arms are still equipped with the type.

Early post-war feats included a flight of six ski and JATO equipped R4Ds launched from an aircraft carrier in support of Admiral Byrd's Antarctic research in 1947. The R4D continued to support 'Deep Freeze' operations for many years, whilst one was the first aircraft to land at the South Pole. This was in 1956 and earlier a USAF C-47 had landed at the North Pole. The US Army operated 30 odd R4D/C-47s up to the 1960s and the US Coast Guard used just a handful.

The Super DC-3 appeared in 1950, but after evaluation by the airlines and the USAF was only accepted by the US Navy, some 100 early R4D models being converted. Armstrong Siddeley tested their Mamba turbo-prop in a Dakota in 1949, followed by Rolls-Royce with the Dart. In the USA, Conroy, twenty years later, fitted both a DC-3 and a Super DC-3 with the Dart turbo-prop, and later with the smaller PT-6 engine. Today the Turbo Express is being evaluated.

The longevity of the DC-3 is a phenomenon which has amazed the air transport world. Rumour has it that future service could depend, not on the DC-3, but very much on the supply of available grades of aviation fuel at an economical price. It is estimated that 1,500 DC-3s including a handful of Super DC-3s are still flying, plus over 100 preserved on display. The future will see the Grand 'Ole Lady soldiering on for some years to come.

(Opposite Top)
A camouflaged RAF Transport Command Dakota seen in final landing sequence at Croydon Airport, Surrey. As a basis for future post-war airline operations, No. 110 Wing and No. 46 Group RAFTC, commenced daily Croydon to Paris, Brussels and Lyon services on September 21, 1944. The Dakotas were drawn from No. 147 Squadron. Subsequently the Lyons service was extended to Marseille and Naples, and new services commenced to Athens, Prague, Warsaw, Copenhagen and Olso using Dakota transports. The author visited Croydon during August 1946 when all No. 110 Wing Dakotas were coded 'CMV' Croydon, Munich, Vienna — followed by three numerals. For example: KG748 CMV-119.

(Opposite Bottom)
In the last phases of World War 2, both in the European and Japanese theatres, the VIP Dakotas from No. 24 Squadron followed up closely behind the fighting forces. Although its base was in the United Kingdom at RAF Hendon just north of London, the squadron carried its VIPs to vital points all over the globe as the battle progressed. Among other duties carried out by the squadron at this time was the movement of doctors and commissions to the notorious German concentration camps scattered around Europe. Photograph shows a typical airfield apron scene at Prague, Czechoslovakia with Douglas Dakotas and Short Stirlings of RAF Transport Command parked after arrival from the United Kingdom.

This early post-war photograph, taken at Schiphol airport, Amsterdam, shows Dutch, Swiss and British Dakota transports parked. The majority of the KLM aircraft still carry the camouflage from their service period when they served with No. 1316 Dutch Communication Flight operating out of the United Kingdom. PH-TBE with the right hand door is an original 1938 built DC-3 which escaped to the UK when the Germans invaded the Netherlands in May 1940. During the post-war period KLM operated nearly 50 Douglas DC-3 transports.

Dakota Mk. IV KK138 'S' for Sugar from No. 1 Parachute Training School located at RAF Upper Heyford in Oxfordshire, seen on a post-war parachute training sortie over the dropping zone at Weston-on-the-Green. The school moved to Upper Heyford from RAF Ringway — now Manchester Airport — during March 1946, and the unit was responsible for the training of large numbers of World War 2 Allied paratroops and instructors, plus many Allied resistance personnel.

After World War 2 Douglas continued taking orders for the commercial DC-3 at the Santa Monica factory, and produced 40 from military transports of which the last one was delivered to Sabena, OO-AWH in 1946. Unfortunately this historic aircraft crashed at London Airport on March 2, 1948. A number of these late models came to Europe to Swissair, Air France, Scandinavian Airlines, Aer Lingus, Sabena, whilst just one late model DC-3 was ordered for the West Indies Division of KLM — Royal Dutch Airlines — the World's Oldest Airline and one of the Douglas company's best customers, having operated every Douglas Commercial from the DC-2 through to the DC-10. Shown is PJ-ALD *Decla* of KLM.

No aeroplane used by the US Army Air Forces has been more widely known, and probably none has been more widely used for so long an operational life, than the Douglas C-47. Produced in greater numbers than any other Army transport, the 'Gooney Bird' was used in every combat theatre of World War 2. More than 1,000 remained in the USAF inventory in 1961. In 1953, all non-standard VC-47 staff transports were redesignated Douglas C-117C, these being the last examples of the military DC-3 to be designated by US services. They were still in service in 1962.

Photograph shows a C-117C originally built in June 1942 as a C-47 Skytrain which served overseas, including North Africa, for three years before returning to the USA. The arrow emblem on the tail has 'NAAMA' indicating it could be the VIP transport of the Commanding General of one of the many huge air material areas within the US. Each window has curtains. From May 1947 to March 1952 the transport was leased to Pioneer Airlines as N47996 *Ben Milan*.

When the Berlin Airlift began in June 1948, there were less than 100 US Air Force C-47s based in Europe, most of them belonging to the European Air Transport Service — EATS. The rest were based with the 60th Troop Carrier Group based at Kaufbeuren Air Base, equipping the 10th, 11th and 12th Troop Carrier Squadrons. On June 26, 1948, 32 Douglas C-47s from Wiesbaden Air Base carried 80 tons of vitally needed supplies into Templehof Air Base in the heart of the now beseiged city.

On that same date, the RAF also began support of the airlift from bases in the British Zone of West Germany. Six Douglas Dakotas, airborne under an Operational Order known as 'Knicker', provided the pattern upon which the most colossal air operation in history was built. Depicted is a night shot of a USAF C-47 Skytrain being marshalled to a halt at Templehof Air Base.

Typical Berlin Airlift scene with a RAF Dakota being loaded with coal by German labour. One RAF Dakota at Wunstorf was loaded in error with a load destined for an Avro York four-engined transport. Respective loads were 5,500 lbs Dakota and 11,500 lbs York. The error was sensed soon after the Dakota pilot made his take-off run, and with great relief to all he missed the perimeter fence. The pilot was requested to return, his reply is unprintable but nothing was going to stop him delivering his extra than normal load to Berlin.

It was an RAF Dakota — KK128 — from Lubeck, which had the distinction of carrying the one millionth ton into Berlin during July 1949. There were problems which were quickly solved. Dakotas being serviced had a considerable layer of coal dust and flour under the floorboards which was taking vital man-hours to remove. Joints in the floorboard were sealed with plasticine which was completely effective.

The Berlin Airlift involved many civil contractors both in providing Dakotas and in providing overhaul facilities for the many military Dakotas. Scottish Aviation at Prestwick Airport alone were responsible for the overhaul of more than 70 RAF Dakotas involved in the airlift, many of which had been in storage since the end of World War 2. In Germany, ex-Luftwaffe hangars at bases like Wunstorf were used for engine overhauls as seen in this photograph.

The United States Air Force personnel from the 86th Tactical Fighter Wing based at Neubiberg air base in West Germany with Republic P-47 Thunderbolt fighters, decided during the period of the Berlin Airlift that they would ensure that the children of West Berlin would not be without toys at Christmas. This Douglas C-47 Skytrain — Oklahoma City built — from the 86th Air Base Group, was used to airlift the gifts into Templehof airfield, West Berlin, and as seen in this photograph was appropriately inscribed. It had been intended to include a young camel for the children, but unfortunately it died.

During the early post-war years, the airlines were always on the lookout for making improvements to their aircraft and service, as competition was heavy, especially in the USA. One such airline was Eastern Air Lines who operated over 60 DC-3s in their fleet, aptly known as the 'The Great Silver Fleet'. They installed this air-stair door that functioned as passenger steps, cabin door, and advertised the flight number and destination. In addition a larger cargo door was also fitted, both modifications giving speedier loading and unloading. Dorothe Bergquist, an EAL secretary from Miami is seen testing the new air-stair door and showing the fashion of that post-war period.

EAL
THE GRE
SILVER FLE
EASTERN
AIR LINES
FLIGHT 152
DESTINATION
CHICAGO
EASTERN AIR LINES
EASTERN
AIR LINE

Founded on March 5, 1937, All American Airways was to pioneer a highly specialised mail service. This incorporated the use of devices for dropping and picking up mail in flight and by this means, no less than fifty-eight small communities in Pennsylvania, Delaware, Maryland, West Virginia and Ohio received a mail service from September 13, 1938, when the airline commenced operations, until June 1949 when the service ceased. By this time the airline had become a normal certificated local carrier. In 1951 the airlines name was changed to Allegheny Airlines. This photograph depicts an early DC-3 transport of All American Airways.

After World War 2 huge stocks of military C-47 transports and spares were to be found surplus to requirement by the Allies at various depots strung across the globe. After conversion these transports served as the back-bone to many of the early post-war airlines of the world. This DC-3 of Jugoslovenski Aero Transport is a good example, being built at Oklahoma City during 1942 for the Royal Air Force as FZ651; one of nearly 2,000 Dakotas obtained under Lend-Lease. In this excellent landing photograph the large cargo doors are very evident.

Shortly after World War 2 a flood of survey and mapping contracts for the world's major continents extended the life of a variety of converted military aircraft, including Dakotas. In 1947 the Canadian Cabinet Defence Committee took on an ambitious long-range programme: a map of all Canada at 1:250,000 scale — about four miles to the inch — in twenty years. By the end of 1967 the programme, to the NATO standard scale 1:250,000 was complete. The mapping at the most useful military scale 1:50,000 was to follow.

Large overseas contracts were issued to survey companies in Canada, the United States and the United Kingdom. Spartan Air Services based in Ottawa was just one of the many companies involved, and this photograph shows Dakota CF-ICU at Dar-es-Salaam, Tanganyika, during a mapping project which is inscribed on the nose of the transport 'Tanzania — Canada S.C.A.A.P. Mapping Project'. The aircraft, ex-Miami Airlines, was built at Long Beach in 1943 as a C-47A-80-DL.

RCAF Dakotas were employed as cargo carriers into snow and ice-covered areas along the Mid-Canada Line, the early warning radar network which roughly follows the fifty-fifth parallel. The Daks operated out of such 'glamorous' bases as Frobisher Bay, Yellowknife, Whitehorse, Goose Bay, Churchill and Thule, often flying from improvised landing strips on the frozen snow.

The winter of 1946/47 was a very cold one and 82°F below zero was recorded at Snag. A Dakota was landed at the Watson Lake airstrip at 50°F below zero. This photograph shows Dakota Mk. III KG414 of the RCAF using RATOG bottles for assisted take-off. During World War 2 this transport served in the United Kingdom with 48 Squadron, being transferred to the RCAF in August 1946, and was one of eight Dakotas donated to the Indian Air Force in November 1962.

There appears to be no end to the Grand 'Ole Lady's talents, either in the air or on the ground, serving the community in many odd ways. In Finland a DC-2 of the Finnish Air Force, after its last flight in April 1955, was preserved as a coffee house at Lakeside Square, Hameenlinna, and is now being restored in a museum. In South Africa rumour has it that a DC-3 snack-bar was completely refurbished and flown again, after 20 years on the ground.

Today, way up north beneath the towering snow-clad peaks of the Himalayas can be found the *Orient Skyliner* a DC-3 fuselage known as the Shangrila Hotel located at Skardu in northern Pakistan. In Australia McDonalds, the hamburger chain, are putting the DC-3 to good use — on the ground of course. This photograph shows an ex-Naval Air Transport Service — NATS — R4D transport somewhere in the USA serving the public as a snack bar shortly after World War 2.

After World War 2, when most combat types were retired to silent rest in weed-choked storage areas, the military DC-3 was assigned the task of filling the need of civil transport demands during the years from late 1945 to 1947 when the larger four-engined types took over on the airlines. A war-weary C-47 could be reconverted to airline luxury in 20 days, costing 20,000 dollars against the pre-war 120,000 dollars new.

This twin-engined jack-of-all-trades helped to make money for the big air freight operators, and money for the odd-ball operators as well. There was little she could not carry, and almost no place she could not go. Fresh fish, fresh produce, furniture, flowers, animals, birds, clams, clothes — a wide variety of cargo still rides in her cabin, much of it refrigerated. The Flying Tiger Line is today one of the world's largest freight hauliers by air transport. Seen at San Francisco Airport in 1946, is an early transport of Flying Tiger appropriately adorned with its shark nose emblem. The converted C-47 is NC59699.

On September 19, 1944, seventeen Dakotas from RAF Down Ampney took off for a third resupply mission to Arnhem, after a delay due to poor visibility. One of the aircraft was KG374, coded YS-L for Love, from 271 Squadron flown by its thirty-year-old captain, Flight Lieutenant David S. A. Lord. He was accompanied by Flying Officer H. A. King (navigator), "Dickie" Medhurst, Alec Ballantyne and four Army despatchers from 223 Company RASC.

After flying for almost two hours, they broke through cloud above the Lower Rhine and were immediately hit by flak. The starboard engine burst into flames but Lord, on hearing that the Dropping Zone was only four minutes away decided to continue. Descending to 900 feet, the aircraft was again hit by flak and the starboard wing caught fire. All but two panniers of ammunition were dropped out of the blazing Dak, so Lord flew round a second perilous time to release the remainder. The Germans automatically concentrated their attack on this flying inferno, battering it with flak. Lord ordered the crew to bale out, desperately trying to fly the Dak straight and level to facilitate their departure. But as they were struggling to attach their parachutes the starboard wing collapsed and fell away.

Harry King was thrown clear of the aircraft and miraculously survived. The rest of the crew perished as the aircraft crashed in flames. Flight Lieutenant David Lord, was posthumously awarded the Victoria Cross on November 13, 1945, for displaying "Supreme valour and self-sacrifice". This was the one and only VC awarded in Transport Command. Today Aces High operates one of its five Dakotas as KG374 YS-L in the livery of David Lord's aircraft. This photograph is featured not only as a tribute to the gallant crews of Transport Command, but to the late Stephen Piercy, friend of the author and friend of many, who took this magnificent photograph. The aircraft carries the registration G-DAKS, and as G-AGHY *Vera* was featured in the TV film series *Airline* titled 'Jack Ruskin Air Services.'

On March 10, 1982, two Transavia Boeing 737 captains founded the Dutch Dakota Association — DDA. On June 27, 1983, the newly-formed DDA made a bid for a 40-year-old Douglas DC-3C, ex-Finnish Air Force DO-7, ex-OH-LCB *Kuikka,* an original Long Beach built C-47A. Negotiations were completed on August 10, 1983, with the Finnish Airline Karair completing a major overhaul and the transport being officially registered PH-DDA on June 10, 1984.

On Friday April 13, 1984, the newly acquired DC-3 had her first test flight after overhaul at Helsinki. Four days later the ferry flight to Holland commenced with a 6 hour 44 min flight to Bremen, where after a night stop it was flown to Amsterdam, to be greeted on the Dutch border by two General Dynamic F-16 Fighting Falcon jets of the Royal Netherlands Air Force. Nearer Amsterdam PH-DDA was escorted by four Fokker S-11 Instructor trainers plus a lone North American T-6 Harvard. Hewlett Packard, an electronic and computer firm support DDA financially so in return have their name on the DC-3. Finnair spent 300 man hours cleaning and painting the veteran with no charge, so their name appears on the aircraft. This fine photograph of PH-DDA was donated by the Dutch Dakota Association and was taken over the Dutch village of Volendam.

This beautifully refurbished and refurnished DC-3 — N711Y — was built at
Oklahoma City for the USAAF, and after World War 2 served with REAL in
Brazil, then with two private owners in the USA before the rock singer Jerry
Lee Lewis purchased it, and at great expense had it modified including new
wings, panoramic windows and a VIP interior to seat 18 passengers. In 1974
Kip du Pont of Summit Aviation, Delaware bought the aircraft which had
26,000 hours on the airframe. Today the aircraft is based at Burbank
Airport, California with the Century Equipment Company. It cruises at 180
mph using 100 gallons of 100 octane fuel per hour. Insurance for such an
aircraft is today 1,600 dollars per year, and the price of a DC-3 ranges from
24,500 dollars to 45,000 dollars, dependent on the condition. In this
photograph N711Y is seen flying over the beauty of the Californian
coastline.

After a very sentimental journey, DC-3 VR-HDB *Betsy,* returns to Hong Kong from Sydney, Australia, along the route she first flew for Cathay Pacific some 37 years and 40,000 flying hours ago. During that time she has used up over 80 new or overhauled Pratt & Whitney radial engines. The USAAF history of *Betsy* is still very vague, but she was a Long Beach C-47 Skytrain completed in June 1942, serving overseas until August 1943, declared surplus in October 1945 and purchased by Ral Farrell a year later when Cathay Pacific was formed becoming VR-HDB on October 3, 1946. Sold as VH-MAL in August 1953, *Betsy* had served the outback of Queensland for ten years, carrying all kinds of cargo where air transport is often the only option. Food supplies, building materials, mining equipment, freshly-caught seafood from the Gulf of Carpentaria, even household furniture, is carried by air. Because of her long fuel endurance and wide door for dropping supplies, *Betsy* had also taken part in numerous Search & Rescue operations. As one of the hundreds of airlines all over the world which owe their existence to the incredible DC-3, Air Queensland, the last owner was delighted at Cathay Pacific's decision to install this trusty transport as a permanent monument to its noble breed.

The entry of the United States into World War 2 during 1941 greatly intensified the problem of aerial rescue, with more aircraft being used on operational missions and so more aircrews requiring assistance. Initially no facilities existed to accomplish rescue missions. As World War 2 developed, Emergency Rescue Squadrons were formed in most theatres equipped with a variety of aircraft.

By March 1945, a total of 1,972 US aircrew had been saved by the British and US rescue forces from the waters surrounding the United Kingdom. In the Spring of 1946 the US Air Rescue Service — ARS — was established as a technical service of the huge US Air Transport Command and one of the types chosen for the service was the Douglas SC-47 Skytrain. This photograph shows a late model SC-47D from Detachment Six of an undesignated Air Rescue Squadron and based at Hamilton Field near San Francisco, captured by the camera on June 23, 1948. The US Coast Guard also used the C-47 Skytrain for air rescue.

Busy apron scene at Manchester Airport which as Ringway was the home of
the Parachute Training School during World War 2. Dakota 'Tango Bravo'
is being prepared for a scheduled flight to Jersey in the Channel Islands. As
an RAF Dakota Mk. IV KN273 it arrived in the United Kingdom from the
USA in February 1945, and served briefly with No. 575 Squadron at Bari,
Italy. In 1946 it went to the Middle East serving with No. 204 Squadron at
Kabrit in the Canal Zone until 1949. It was ferried to No. 22 MU at Silloth in
September 1950. After conversion as a civil Dakota G-ANTB it served with
Transair, Alares Development Co. and finally British United. It crashed at
Jersey on April 14, 1965.

(Opposite)

After World War 2 and the Berlin Airlift which followed, hundreds of RAF Dakotas became surplus and were stored at three main Maintenance Units in the United Kingdom. These were No. 8 MU at Little Rissington, No. 12 MU at Kirkbride and No. 22 at Silloth.

The UK weather took toll of the exterior of these wartime transports as can be seen by this Dakota still in ferry makings which had been in storage at No. 12 MU from October 1949 until April 1953. Its wartime service had included periods in the Middle East and with ACSEA — Air Command South-east Asia. When No. 114 Squadron was reformed on August 1, 1947 at Kabrit in the Middle East KJ998 served with the unit until 1949. After conversion by Aviation Services the transport went to Hunting-Clan and two months later to Eagle Aviation, but not for long. In January 1953 it was sold to Central African Airways and was last heard of with Air Rhodesia.

British European Airways was formed on August 1, 1946, with several DC-3s on lease from BOAC, and by 1956 had a fleet of over 50 which operated until 1962 when the last one was sold. Wartime restrictions on civil flying in the United Kingdom were revoked on January 1, 1946, and on that day the British European Airways Division of BOAC was formed to take over the services operated by No. 110 Wing of RAF Transport Command from Croydon.

It was not until March 4, 1946, that the BEA Division began operating under civil markings, the crews wearing BOAC uniform. G-AHCZ was a Mk. III built at Oklahoma City and delivered to BOAC in April 1946. It was transferred to BEA on August 13, 1947, and named *Charles Samson* and became a Pionair Class DC-3 with modifications including an air-stair door. It flew the last BEA service between Northolt and Jersey on October 30, 1954. With 19,958 hours on the airframe it was transferred to Cambrian Airways on March 2, 1959.

The two Dart Dakotas operated by British European Airways between 1951 and 1953 were the first turbine-powered aircraft to be placed in revenue-earning airline service anywhere in the world. These were G-ALXN *Sir Henry Royce* and G-AMDB *Claude Johnson* both converted for BEA by Field Aircraft Services at Tollerton to prove the Rolls-Royce Dart engine in commercial use before the introduction of the Viscount in 1952.

The Twin Wasp engines on the BEA aircraft were replaced by 1,400 shp (plus 365 lbs of jet thrust) Dart R.Da 3/505 turboprop engines in 1951. The first scheduled cargo service was flown by G-ALXN on the Northolt to Hannover route on August 15, 1951. They cruised normally at a true air speed of 207 mph at 26,000 feet on a total of 1,300 shp with a fuel consumption of 900 lb/hr. In all the two Dakotas flew some 5,319 hours in BEA service up to March 1953 when the transports were converted back to standard Pratt & Whitney Wasp aircraft.

A Dakota Mk. IV — KJ839 — ex-RAF Transport Command, with low airframe hours and unfurnished, was selected by Armstrong Siddeley to have its Pratt & Whitney Twin Wasps replaced by the company's new Mamba turboprops. Scottish Aviation at Prestwick were largely involved with the modification work and the first flight took place at Bitteswell near Rugby on August 27, 1959.

The Mamba ASM 3 turboprops each produced 1,475 equivalent shaft horsepower. Test pilot was Waldo Price-Owen who flew the Mamba Dakota many hours on test-bed research. The Dakota was built at Oklahoma City for the RAF and arrived in the United Kingdom in September 1944 serving with No. 147 Squadron and a couple of Dakota Conversion Units before going to Armstrong Siddeley. During 1958 the Twin Wasps were re-installed and the aircraft sold to Salmesbury Engineering, later going to Skyways of London and Bahama Airways.

Using radio call-sign 'Victor 4' Douglas R4D-5 BuNo. 17238 launches off the aircraft carrier *USS Philippine Sea* CVA-47 at 1844 GMT on January 29, 1947, using its four JATO bottles to assist take-off. A carrier take-off in any aircraft was a new experience for most Operation High Jump pilots, as not more than two had previous carrier experience.

Each transport carried five passengers and the varied gear was equalised to give each transport the same load. Crew members were limited to 15 lbs. of baggage. The landing skis were developed by the Federal Aircraft works in Minneapolis and trials were carried out in the snow fields of Montana. The skis increased the weight of the R4D by 1,105 lbs. When flying was terminated for the season the six transports had to be left at the Little America base.

The US Navy's 'Operation High Jump', with 13 ships and 4,000 men was the largest Antarctic expedition ever organised. Led by Admirals Richard E. Byrd and Richard H. Cruzen, it photographed most of the continent's coastline during 1946-47. Six Douglas R4D-5 transports were included in the 26 aircraft which made up the armada. Fitted with JATO bottles these Douglas transports took off from the aircraft carrier *USS Philippine Sea* and landed safely at Little America IV, a base 600 miles distant from the carrier. Framed by the implements of the Antarctic, two of the six Douglas R4D-5 transports are seen parked at the Little America base. It was found that although the ski-wheel combination had accomplished its purpose, three inches of wheel protruding through the skis caused excessive drag when taxying on snow. Therefore the wheels were removed from all six aircraft.

Excellent side profile of Douglas R4D-8L (Super DC-3) BuNo. 17219 named *Semper Shafters USMC* flying above the rugged Antarctic terrain between Byrd Station and McMurdo. The landing gear had collapsed whilst landing in Horlicks Mountains. With the undercarriage temporarily repaired the transport was flown with gear down to Byrd Station and then to the US Naval Air Facility at McMurdo Sound. During the flight it was overtaken by a Douglas R4D-5 transport BuNo. 17246 named *Little Horrible – Korora II 1960* and given an escort home.

Scene at McMurdo Sound air base, Antarctica on January 10, 1957. Three Douglas R4D-5 transports from the US Navy VX-6 Squadron — XD/1 *Korara II*, XD/8 *Que Sera Sera* and XD/7 *Takahe*. At 0834 GMT on October 31, 1956, *Que Sera Sera* made the first landing at the South Pole. Admiral Dufek stepped from the Douglas transport, the first man to stand at the South Pole since Amundsen and Scott. He was struck by the intense cold, 58°F below zero that was intensified by a 10/15 knot wind.

The crew spent 49 minutes on the ground before returning to their base at Beardmore Scott. The Douglas transport served faultlessly with 'Operation Deep Freeze' throughout the years until 1968 when the type was at last retired by VX-6 from Antarctic skies. *Que Sera Sera* had become a marked aircraft, and when its Antarctic days were over, the US Navy graciously retired it to their museum located at Pensacola, Florida during December 1958.

This US Air Force ski-equipped Douglas C-47 Skytrain, seen elevated on a 30-feet high mound of ice above the main body of Ice Station Bravo, made a forced landing on the ice island during the mid fifties. The transport was cannibilized leaving only the shell on the wind-eroded mound of ice. Ice Station Bravo, also known as 'T for Tango 3', is located 95 miles North of Point Barrow, Alaska, and from 1952 until late 1961, was used as a USAF weather station and scientific outpost. The unit was disbanded during late September 1961, when the 2,500 ft. runway and eventually the ice-cap, began to break-up and drift away. The C-47 guardian of the island sank to the bottom of the ocean.

Typical post-war factory scene, in this case at the Scottish Aviation facility at Prestwick Airport, Scotland, in January 1967. The craftsmen involved had probably worked on the Dakota during World War 2. Wings were removed and 'pulled' at the appropriate stage in the hour life of the transport. At one stage the US Civil Aeronautics Board — CAB — made attempts to ground the Grand 'Ole Lady on account of her age, but without success.

In the United Kingdom, Hants and Sussex Aviation, located at Portsmouth Airport, held a world-wide reputation for their overhaul and rebuild of the Pratt & Whitney Twin Wasp engines which powered the DC-3 Dakota. Many DC-3s now flying are powered by the more powerful 2,000 hp Twin Wasp as fitted to the larger DC-4 Skymaster.

West Coast Airlines of Seattle, though founded on March 14, 1941, was not certified until May 22, 1946, flying its first service with DC-3s on December 5 of that year. It flew a service from Seattle to Portland and Medford in Oregon. On August 4, 1952, it absorbed Empire Air Lines and on April 17, 1968, merged with Bonanza and Pacific to form Air West. This photograph of a West Coast DC-3 gives an excellent view of the two Pratt & Whitney Twin Wasp engines, the Hamilton Standard hydromatic propellers, the undercarriage and the nose section.

During the 1950s, sporadic studies were made in Europe and the USA for what became known as a 'DC-3, replacement'. There were many contending designs put forward but the DC-3 remained in a class of its own in the world of 3,000 ft. runways, at altitudes up to 8,000 ft. and in temperatures up to 120°F. Conditions which were all too common in the US on the networks of operators like Frontier Airlines, West Coast Airlines and Bonanza.

One airline, Lake Central, went as far as to study the possibility of putting the DC-3 back into production, with improvements, but was shocked to discover how much a new DC-3 would cost. The DC-3 may have been well worn, but the initial cost was so low that shortcomings in design of both airframe and engines were more than compensated for. It was evident that nothing could match the DC-3 for local service. Quote: 'The only replacement for a DC-3 is another DC-3'. Unquote. Photograph illustrates N18667, a war surplus Santa Monica built C-53D Skytrooper, a model which had just one single passenger door.

The three main airlines of New Zealand, Union Airways, Air Travel and Cook Strait Airways amalgamated on December 7, 1945 to form New Zealand National Airways Corporation. DC-3s replaced smaller aircraft types on the major routes, and these formed the backbone of the fleet until replacement by Viscounts in February 1958. *Skyliner Whakatane* is shown. It was an Oklahoma City built C-47 for the Royal New Zealand Air Force. Surplus to requirements it was acquired by NZNAC initially as *Flagship Papango* and after 1958 went to Mount Cook & Southern Lakes Tourist Co. Ltd., later Mount Cook Airlines.

Avianca, the national airline of Colombia, used some 40 DC-3s, many acquired in April 1954, when it absorbed Lansa the largest Colombian carrier. This photograph shows HK-118 an early Long Beach built C-47 military transport completed in December 1942, which was declared surplus in March 1946 after USAAF service. It is one of several Avianca DC-3 transports marked Hi-Per indicating they were fitted with the more powerful DC-4 engines which had been purchased from Pan American Airways. On October 17, 1965, HK-118 was involved in a mid-air collision with a Piper light aircraft over Gomex Nino Airport, Bucaramanga, Colombia and was written off.

Comapana Mexicana de Aviacion (CMA) was founded in Mexico City on August 20, 1924, by two US citizens to carry payrolls on a charter basis throughout the oilfields near Tampico. During World War 2, CMA became affiliated to Pan American and until the late 1940s was the largest airline in Mexico. Compared with most, its fleet was comparatively modern, with DC-3s opening a route to Havana in October 1942. A connection to the Guatamalan frontier, at Tapachula, and a second route to the US border, at Nuevo Laredo, was opened in 1943.
XA-FEG was a Pratt & Whitney Twin Wasp powered DC-3A model 414 purchased by Pan American from the Defence Supply Corporation in February 1942 for CMA use. It was last seen derelict at Mexico City in September 1976.

A combination of Western Air Express, General Air Lines and National Park Airways, the company took the name Western Air Lines on April 17, 1941. It was one of the airlines which mounted an Alaskan ferrying operation during World War 2. Most of its DC-3 equipment was taken over by the government during the war, and the company flew one of the most difficult supply routes from Great Falls, Montana to Fairbanks and Nome, Alaska, via Edmonton, Alberta. In spite of one of the worst winters in recorded history, when even the southernmost point of the route experienced temperatures of minus 40°F., Western maintained a perfect safety record. The DC-3, NC18600, in this photograph was a USAAF C-53 Skytrooper procured by Western on August 1, 1949.

When the BAC Concorde flight-test unit was established at RAF Fairford, Gloucestershire, during the late 1960s, by the British Aircraft Corporation, a suitable aircraft was required to transport personnel, supplies etc to and from the BAC factory located at Filton, Bristol. A British registered Douglas Dakota G-AMPO was purchased for £28,000, commencing a ferry service during December 1969. Over nearly three years the transport flew 1,672 hours mainly on the Filton - Fairford - Filton route. The Dakota was sold on August 17, 1972 for £12,000 to Macedonia. The aircraft was a Oklahoma City built C-47B Dakota serving with No. 238 Squadron RAF during 1945, being eventually sold as surplus to requirements in February 1952 when it went to Starways.

The Southern African Air Force has the proud distinction of operating the Douglas C-47 Skytrain since the first day of June 1943, when No. 28 Squadron was formed with the motto 'Portamus — We Carry' operating under the RAF 216 Group in the Middle East. The first entry in the operational record book reads 'In humble surroundings at SAAF Base Depot, Almaza, Cairo, Middle East: 28 Squadron is born'.

By September 1943 the unit had detachments based at Pachino, Sicily: Lecce, Italy: Oudja, Morocco and Setif, Algeria, with a detachment later moving to Bari, Italy during November. By the end of April 1944, 28 Squadron was equipped with 30 Dakotas, and during that year a total of 87,029 passengers and 33,692,361 lbs. of freight were carried and total flying hours for the year amounted to 38,859. A second Squadron, No. 44, was later formed, both squadrons being heavily involved in the Balkan campaign. Today the Douglas transport serves in unknown numbers with South Africa, assisting in many clandestine operations in the war in Angola and Namibia.

Through the good offices of the South African Air Force, Louis J. Vosloo was allowed a special air-to-air photographic sortie with Dakota 6858 for photographs to be used exclusively in this tribute. The Dak was from 25 Squadron based at Ysterplaat, Cape Town, and the photographs were taken over the beautiful shoreline of the Cape Peninsular. The wartime numbered unit 44 Squadron still exists with Dakotas at Swartkop, Pretoria, and 86 Advanced Flying School at Bloemspruit still operates the type. In 1971 five ex-South African Airways DC-3s were impressed into use with the SAAF.

The 30th Anniversary of the end of the Berlin Airlift was celebrated on May 12, 1979, with an 'Open House' at the USAF base at Templehof in the heart of the city. The last remaining Dakota in RAF livery, KG661, operated by the Ministry of Defence at RAE Farnborough was one of the aircraft invited, with the author as one of the crew members. This photograph, taken from an Army Air Corps Gazelle helicopter, has captured the Dak on final approach to Templehof, a flight plan flown by sister Dakota transports during the busy days of the airlift.

Described appropriately as the world's gaudiest Dakota aircraft — a dazzling confection of black and yellow stripes seen on Dakota 6877. It has been towing aerial targets for anti-aircraft gunners for more than 20 years and has finally shed its coat of eye-catching colours. In June 1984, 6877 emerged from a major refit in sober camouflage joining her camouflaged colleagues of No. 25 Squadron, South African Air Force, Ysterplaat Air Base, Cape Town.

This Dakota was built at Oklahoma City in 1942 for the Royal Air Force, was transferred to the SAAF and entered service as a target-tug in 1960, when it received the new striped look. This was necessary to avoid unfortunate mistakes during target practice. Despite a new generation of anti-aircraft weapons making her bright colours obsolete, a new target-tug — Dakota 6858 — has been introduced. Dakota 6877 has flown for nearly quarter of a century with characteristic Dak reliability.

Today the Turkish Air Force — Turk Hava Kuvvetleri — THK — is the mainstay of the 6th Allied Tactical Air Force under NATO's Allied Air Forces Southern Europe, and is the most easterly NATO member. On May 22, 1947, US Congress gave its approval of 400 million dollars of which 26,750,000 was for the THK. Further dollar aid in 1948 was followed by a US Military Air Mission, plus US airfield construction engineers who commenced modernisation and extension of Turkish bases.

The first Douglas C-47 transports were included in the re-equipping and modernisation of the THK. Turkey became a NATO member in 1952, and is strategically important, having a common border with the USSR, and also controlling the Dardanelle and Bosporus Straits. The THK C-47s were used in anger during the invasion of Cyprus during July 1974, dropping paratroops. Today some 40 C-47s are still in use equipping support squadrons at Yesilkoy, Ekismesgar, Erzurum, with the 8th VIP Transport Unit. Most air bases have a communication flight utilising at least one Douglas C-47.

Douglas R4D-5, the US Navy equivalent of the C-47 Skytrain, from the Naval Aviation Research Facility — NARF — at Warminster, seen dropping paramedics during an exercise. The US Navy VX-6 Squadron based in the Antarctic during 'Operation Deep Freeze' used para rescue teams on Search and Rescue operations. The team normally consisted of a jump-master, hospital corpsman, parachute rigger and a general specialist. Para-Marines were trained during World War 2 at the US Marine Corps station at Cheery Point, South Carolina, using Douglas transports. After use with the NARF the aircraft in the photograph was placed in storage at Davis-Monthan, Arizona.

'Old Dakotas never die'. During 1954 a type of reverse Lend-Lease project involving approximately 150 RAF Dakotas was launched, the transports being reconditioned at US expense by Field Aircraft Services, and then returned for use by NATO forces within Europe including the US Air Force. The Dakotas, in a derelict state due to the UK weather, had been stored at three maintenance units, one in Gloucestershire and two in Cumberland. The refurbishing of each aircraft up to flight test, took approximately one year, after which the shiny C-47 appeared in USAF livery. The project was completed in July 1956.

The French overnight Postal Service was operated by a fleet of 20 Air France owned DC-3s and crews, who every night, no matter what the weather — rain, snow, ice, fog — delivered the mail to the four corners of France. When other aircraft were grounded due to weather conditions the mail DC-3 transports flew as normal. After World War 2, in 1946, the service was introduced initially using Junkers Ju-52 transports, then the DC-3.

Statistics showed a near 100 per cent reliability, an example being 1963 when during 11,800 landings at night, there were only two that missed, both because the runways at Strasbourg were coated with ice and there was a cross wind of 50 knots. When the unique Postal Service disposed of its DC-3s, two were sold to a transport company based in Florida. The ferry pilot who collected them flew them both back to Miami, solo.

During the Malayan anti-terrorist campaign — 'Operation Firedog' — a detachment of Dakotas from No. 41 Squadron Royal New Zealand Air Force, was involved for over three years. In this photograph a New Zealand Air Force Dakota is on a supply dropping mission over the dense Malayan jungle during July 1950. The Skytrain is a very late model built at Oklahoma City during 1945. It was only during 1977 that thoughts for a Dakota replacement came about, and the final retirement ceremony took place on November 12, 1977 at Ohakea when the log books of the last two C-47 Dakotas were ceremoniously handed over to the Chief of the Air Staff to the lament of a lone piper, ending 34 years of faithful Dakota service.

Vietnam AC-47 Spooky gunship missions were often supported by Douglas EC-47/P/Q transports with their electronic jamming capabilities. In order to generate sufficient power for the increased electronics carried, some of these transports had to be re-engined with the larger Pratt & Whitney R-2000-7 engines, these engines being built for the four-engined Douglas C-54 transport. These unarmed C-47s were also psychological warfare aircraft known as 'Gabby' with a large speaker mounted in the cargo door and an ARVN trooper would talk to the Viet Cong below. Others would cruise over the Viet Cong infested areas along the Republic of Vietnam coast, dropping leaflets designed to persuade insurgents to turn themselves in. During and after the New Year holiday season in January 1966 more than 1,600 Viet Cong defected, using the leaflets as safe conduct passes. Photograph by Norman Taylor depicts a EC-47P-45-DK 45-1046 from the 361st Tactical Electronic Warfare Squadron, 460th Tactical Reconnaissance Wing, over Laos on June 16, 1971

In the 1950s, the Airsearch Company sold a kit which allowed the maximization of the DC-3, that is to give it better performance thanks to more streamlined engine nacelles, and doors for the landing gear. The complete kit also included a new empennage of larger dimensions.

This photograph shows a heavily modified DC-3 transport of Air Madagascar, one of a fleet of six with which the company was re-formed on the first day of January 1962. The DC-3s were used on domestic routes, and were mainly ex-Air France transports. The origin of DC-3 5R-MAI in the photograph was a Oklahoma City model C-47A-15-DK constructed in 1942 for the US Army Air Force and used by Air France from 1958 onwards.

Photographed in rugged mountainous surroundings at Habalyn airstrip in Aden, during 1966 is RAF Middle East Command Dakota Mk. IV KN452, an Oklahoma City built transport. Fitted out as a freight aircraft, KN452 had previously served with No. 10 Squadron and with the Air Officer Commanding Gibraltar. Many sorties into the Radfan were flown with this aircraft, against the rebel tribesmen from South Yemen. It was replaced with an Andover transport which unfortunately did not serve as well as the Dakota in the rough terrain.

During 1949/50, the Royal Australian Navy took over two ex-Royal Australian Air Force Dakotas, these operating in passenger and cargo configuration. One of these, serial N2-23, was later modified as a flying classroom for the training of de Havilland Sea Venom and Fairey Gannet navigators. The nose was elongated to accommodate radar whilst a further retractable radar was installed in the fuselage just forward of the main cargo door access.

This installation was later removed and the Dakota reverted back to passenger layout. In 1968 a further two Dakota transports were acquired from the RAAF, both operating in the passenger role. By 1977 all the Navy Daks had been phased out of service, two being sold. N2-90 went to *HMAS Nirimba,* west of Sydney, for apprentice training, and the Royal Australian Navy located at *HMAS Albatross,* Nowra, New South Wales, was allocated N2-43 for preservation. Photograph shows radar-equipped Dakota N2-43 at Nowra in the markings 800/NW of No. 851 Squadron Royal Australian Navy.

A great source of USAF strength today is still supplied by the Air National
Guard — ANG — a unique organisation, under the command of the
respective governors of individual states, but also subject to call-up by the
President, Congress, or the provisions of certain US Public Laws. The ANG
operates more than 1,500 aircraft of many types, and represents almost one-
fifth of the total strength of the USAF. Most Air National Guard Wing,
Group and Squadrons had at least one C-47 on strength which was used as a
unit 'hack' to transport equipment and personnel in support of operational
aircraft.

Photographed showing its single-engine capability is a C-47 Skytrain
belonging to the Pennsylvania ANG operating out of its home base of
Pittsburg Airport, Pa. Forty-eight unit training sessions and thirty-six
proficiency flights for aircrew are the annual minimum requirements for
ANG personnel.

Transport ancient and modern come together at the rough but adequate airstrip located at Debre Tabor in the north central part of Ethiopia. A network of airstrips such as this plus airports connect other parts of the country with the capital. With technical advice and DC-3s from Trans World Airlines — TWA — Ethiopian Air Lines was founded on December 21, 1945, operations commencing on April 8, 1946, with a fleet of five Douglas C-47 transports. They operated a local network within Ethiopia and to neighbouring countries. This photograph was taken during 1958 and today, 27 years later DC-3s are still in use and have been involved in transporting food and medicine to famine victims.

Royal Nepal Airlines used five DC-3s on domestic services within Nepal and to India. In the 1960s when Nepal attempted to modernise its economy, both the United Nations and the International Civil Aviation Organisation — ICAO — assisted the Government of Nepal in its programme, by providing experts in civil aviation.

Aircraft such as the DC-3 have proved to be indispensable in the development of a transportation system, in a country that had different parts cut off from each other by the rugged terrain. The aircraft is an ex-military C-47 which can be utilised for either cargo or passengers, at Gorka airstrip in April 1967.

RAF Dakota Mk. III TS423 was one of many used on Research and Development contracts. A Long Beach built glider-tug completed at the end of 1943, it arrived in Europe with the US Eighth Air Force early in 1944 and in September was transferred to the RAF. It joined the Royal Canadian Air Force for use in Burma, after which it returned to Europe and served in Berlin during March 1946. A year later it was in storage with No. 44 Maintenance Unit with only 766 hours on the airframe. For the next few years it was a research platform allotted to Ferranti at Edinburgh. Equipment fitted included a hydraulically-operated gun turret fitted in the nose and Airpass radar as fitted in the English Electric Lightning interceptor. The transport accumulated 1,300 hours on trials. Today it is flying with Aces High Limited in civilian guise, being seen at air shows and in TV films.

This spike-nose specimen of the Douglas DC-3 is wearing the radome of the Lockheed F-104 Starfighter. Registered N18565 it was originally built at Santa Monica as a C-53 Skytrooper and after war service joined the fleet of TWA at Burbank, California with the F-104 nose and equipment. Details were released by Lockheed on November 16, 1960, revealing that inside the Douglas transport was a complete F-104G cockpit mockup, test and measuring equipment permitting in-flight evaluation of the Starfighter's all-weather, advanced radar and fire control equipment. The 8-foot nose spike carried the interchangeable electronics gear, which became standard equipment on hundreds of NATO F-104 fighters then scheduled for delivery to West Germany, the Netherlands, Canada, Belgium and Italy plus non-NATO Japan. In addition many of these NATO air arms equipped their own C-47s with the F-104 equipment and nose. Lockheed flight test teams revealed that the unusual appurtenance had no adverse effect on the venerable DC-3's aerodynamic characteristics. After demonstrations to the NATO countries Lockheed sold N18565 to the German Air Force at Kaufbeuren, West Germany on January 12, 1962. In May 1968 it was surplus to requirements and sold to a firm in Malta.

Today the huge Military Aircraft Storage and Deposition Centre located at Davis-Monthan AFB in Arizona employs nearly 600 civilians, uses most of its 3,000 acres, and has under care some 3,500 aircraft from the US military armed forces. Since 1945, when the unit was established, the Douglas C-47 Skytrain and its many variants has been stored here — in 1946 there were 256 C-47s stored, and a similar number 25 years later, these including the Super DC-3 as used by the US Navy and Marine Corps.

A low rainfall, low humidity, low acidic content plus the hard-baked soil make conditions perfect for either long or short term storage of aircraft. After the Vietnam conflict the numbers in storage increased greatly; seen in this Davis-Monthan photograph is a camouflaged Douglas C-47 O-48579 *Road Runner Airlines* with flower children symbols on the fin.

A variety of uses have been found over the years for surplus military Douglas C-47 Skytrain transports, many brought out of long-term storage at the huge Davis-Monthan storage complex in Arizona. The US Department of Agriculture took a single C-47 plus several larger C-54 transports for use in an experiment to control the screw-worm fly, which plagues cattle in the south-western US. Male flies sterilised by exposure to cobalt rays were dropped from the air in boxes that opened on impact with the ground, in an attempt to curtail breeding of the species. Another Douglas C-47 was used by the City of New Orleans in a highly successful mosquito control programme. Seen parked on a weed-infested parking area at an airport in Florida is a Oklahoma City built C-47, used for mosquito control work.

With no customer for the civil Super DC-3, Douglas turned to the USAF who were at the time looking for a new twin-engined medium range transport. The military version of the Super DC-3 differed in having a large cargo door, a heavier metal floor, and 1,475 hp Wright 1820-80 engines. In addition it was fitted with twin main wheels and was equipped for short field take-off capability with JATO bottles. It was initially designated YC-129, but in recognition of its C-47 origins, it became YC-47F with USAF serial 51-3817.

After extensive tests held at Wright-Patterson, the USAF placed no production order, deciding in favour of the new Convair C-131. In 1951 the YC-47F was turned over to the US Navy to become the R4D-8 in the Navy inventory, ending up with Build No. 138820. Spectacular photograph of the YC-47F taking off from Wright-Patterson assisted by JATO power.

After the end of World War 2, a number of DC-3 replacements appeared on the market, some larger and faster, and all more expensive designs. After rebuilding some surplus C-47s and C-117s as model DC-3C and DC-3D airliners, the Douglas Aircraft Company quickly decided that the only real replacement for the DC-3 would be an improved DC-3 rather than an entirely new design. Consequently, it developed the Super DC-3, which was simply a standard DC-3A with extensive modifications.

The fuselage was lengthened by extending the nose section forward, and the rear compartment aft, giving an effective cabin increase of 79 inches. Larger vertical and horizontal tail surfaces were fitted, the R-1830 engines were replaced by 1,475 hp Wright R-1820-80 engines. The engine nacelles were enlarged to completely enclose the wheels when retracted, the tail wheel was made partially retractable and new and slightly smaller outer wing panels were swept back four degrees at the trailing edge to accommodate the rearward shift of the centre of gravity. Seating was increased to maximum 38. The first flight of the Super DC-3 N30000 took place on 23 June, 1949, designed DC-3S c/n 43158. The original sales idea was for the airline customer to trade in a standard DC-3 and, for a price, get a Super DC-3 in exchange. Only one airline customer was found — Capital Airways who operated three Super DC-3s, these later going to US Steel. This rare photograph shows N16012, the third aircraft.

Turbo Express is a conversion of a Douglas DC-3, by the United States Aircraft Corporation, from conventional piston-driven engines to Pratt & Whitney PT6 turboprop engines which deliver a slightly higher thrust. The new engine installation increases the useful load substantially with less aerodynamic drag. The cruising speed and overall aircraft performance is increased. Modifications include a 40-inch plug fitted in the fuselage forward of the wings, updated avionics, hydraulics and pneumatics, modified control systems, wing strengthening spar caps and attachment strap components. The two 1,245 esph PT6A-45R engines are fitted in new flat-sided lifting nacelles with overwing exhaust systems, and new five-bladed Hartzell aluminium props are used. The wing tips have been squared-off and the leading edge of the outer half span of the wings has been reconfigured and includes a twist to improve stall characteristics. During March 1984, the new DC-3 conversion received its FAA certification and is currently being considered by the Columbian Government for an order for nine aircraft representing 13 million dollars. A company demonstration DC-3 fitted with PT6A-65R engines will provide improved performance at conditions of elevated temperature and high altitude.

After World War 2, Mohawk Airlines introduced a 'Gaslight' service with DC-3s, with the stewardesses dressed in appropriate French chorus girl livery. Thunderbird Texas-Pacific Northwest Express had at least one DC-3 finished in what can only be described as 'totem pole' livery. This gaily-decorated Kwin Air DC-3 N55KN is believed to be still around and operates out of Fort Lauderdale in Florida. It is a 1942 Santa Monica built C-53 Skytrooper which served in the UK and in North Africa before going to TWA in 1945. It went to Mexico in 1950, was back in the USA with the Studebaker Corporation in 1968, and received its gaudy finish in October 1978 when it was sold to the Bird of the Sun Air Travel Club.

Now an annual event in the aviation calendar, is the gigantic air show put on at Harlingen, Texas, by the huge Confederate Air Force organisation. It attracts aviation buffs from all over the globe. This is often a one and only chance to see a rare World War 2 vintage veteran flying. At the 25th Anniversary air show in 1982 some 130 aircraft were included. The transport aircraft section has never been without at least two C-47 Gooney Birds and this beautiful air-to-air photograph of Confederate Air Force C-47 *Buzz Buggy* represents a D-Day C-47 operated by the Ninth Troop Carrier Command.

Two psychedelic Dakotas appeared in Canada during the 1970s, both owned by D. G. Harris Productions Limited, both named *Arctic 7* and one replacing the other. Both were ex-World War 2 Long Beach built Skytrains, the first serving in Alaska with the US Air Transport Command, the other in North Africa. The first *Arctic 7* CF-JRY was possibly the most exotic but was wrecked at Malton Airport, Ontario, on August 29, 1970, when gale force winds of incredible strength flung the transport over on its back. The replacement *Arctic 7* was CF-CSC which, unfortunately, was destroyed by fire on November 15, 1975, at La Grande, Quebec.

DC-3 with a dual role is OH-VKB of Kar-Air in Finland, seen fitted with geophysical survey equipment, yet still retaining its passenger-carrying capability. This DC-3A-214 was assembled by Fokker during August 1937 and delivered to ABA in Sweden as SE-BAC *Falken* during September 1939. In April 1948 it was transferred to SAS as *Folke Viking*. In January 1954 it went to Finland and was retired from active flying in 1979 with 35,475 hours 25 minutes on the airframe. Today it is located at Tampere Airport in custody with the Finnish Aviation Museum Society, being transferred on January 10, 1984.

Sunbird Aviation Limited currently operates two veteran DC-3s on charter and scheduled services out of Wilson Airport, Nairobi. The only two DC-3s registered in Kenya. Their impressive operational performance enables them to be used on virtually all general aviation airfields in the country, and their long-range fuel tanks mean they can tackle any route within Kenya. These Sunbird Dakotas, formerly operated by the defunct East African Airways, have been flying throughout Kenya, Tanzania and Uganda for 34 years and in the words of a veteran ex-EAA and now Sunbird Dak captain, they practically know their way around without a pilot. The DC-3s can carry 36 passengers and fly a twice daily service from Nairobi to Masai Mara mainly with tourists for the game reserves. During 1974, the service carried a few hundred passengers — in 1983 over 15,000 seats were filled. On occasions the seats have been removed to make room for relief food to ease the hardships of hungry people in drought-stricken areas of Northern Kenya. One of the Sunbird veterans — 5Y-AAE — is a 1944 Oklahoma City model which went to the RAF as a Dakota Mk. IV KN418, which served with No. 53 Squadron and with No. 1 Parachute Training School. It was sold to East African Airways on February 25, 1952.

It can be claimed, without much contradiction, that the general outline of the Douglas DC-3 has not changed since the first DST version took to the air on December 17, 1935. Today the wing span remains at 95 ft. and the length at just under 65 ft. During World War 2 it was discovered the fuselage and wings were sufficiently strong to carry supply panniers, and even small bombs. In India spare C-47 wings were ferried strapped below the fuselage. Later in the war, radar bulges appeared, whilst the large roomy fuselage was ideal for carrying anything but what it was designed for.

Today, 50 years later, the DC-3 is still in demand as the ideal aircraft for research and development and survey tasks. In Australia, Canada and South Africa varied fleets of DC-3s are to be found on survey work carrying weird magnetic field anomaly detector gear. In some cases a vast aerial is stretched right around the aircraft from nose to wing-tip to tail to wing-tip and return. This acts as a giant flying electro-magnet which can be used to plot variations in the earth trace to spot potential mineral deposits.

During 1974, General Aviation Services Limited, formed in Jersey during 1969, registered the trading name 'Air Atlantique'. In 1976 the decision to break new ground was made, and two Dakotas were purchased — G-AMCA and G-ANAF — the latter transports commencing general freight and aerial survey throughout Europe. In July 1981, the Dakota fleet was increased to the present fleet of eight and a new base was introduced at Blackpool Airport. Since 1976 the Dakota fleet has flown freighter charters all over Europe, the Mediterranean and Africa carrying such varied cargoes as day-old-chicks, donkeys, motor vehicles parts, and even replacement Rolls-Royce Spey engines for the BAC-111s and Fokker F.28s of several major European and British carriers.

The Dakota has been a workhorse for the United Nations, and since the 1950s has seen stalwart service with UN missions located in Indonesia, Greece, Palestine, India, Pakistan, in the Gaza Strip and Sinai Desert and in the Congo, not to mention a more recent trouble spot — the Lebanon. All these missions have used at least one Dakota transport — the Congo mission had no less than ten in service at one time.

The aircraft has carried freight and passengers, served as an ambulance aircraft and been used for observation. The majority of the Dakotas came from the Canadian Armed Forces inventory, but the USAF, Italian Air Force and other countries have all provided aircraft and crews. This photograph was taken at Gaza airstrip during July 1960 and shows equipment being loaded on to a Dakota bound for the UN Mission in the Congo.

Operated by the Naval Arctic Research Laboratory, Barrow, Alaska, this Douglas C-117D Super DC-3 BuNo. 17156 N722NR, known as *Red Nose* made the most northerly landing by its type at Alert, Ellesmere Island, North West Territories, in support of a US Navy ice station acoustics programme. *Red Nose* subsequently carried out Arctic remote sensing (laser profilometer), infra-red scanning and carries SLAR (sideward-looking radar), as well as carrying out more mundane logistic flights. The SLAR can be seen slung beneath the aircraft looking like an aerial torpedo.

The war in Indochina during the 1950s involved many Dakota units and personnel of the Armee de l'Air or French Air Force. By the end of the war the Franche-Comte group had flown 21,000 combat missions, the Anjou group 17,596 and the Touraine and Bearn groups similar numbers — all with the Douglas C-47 Skytrain. The transport pilots were flying an average of 200 hours per month, sometimes reaching a peak of over 300 hours.

The French Government leased several civil DC-3 transports from private companies such as Autrex and Aigle Azur for carrying supplies to forward bases, whilst the military C-47s dropped paratroops, and supplies as well as evacuating the many wounded. This combat photograph, taken on March 18, 1954, at Dien Bien Phu shows a French Air Force C-47 hospital transport taking off with Vietminh shells exploding on the airstrip. Despite the shelling the photographer kept his shutter clicking.

This DC-3 was originally a Santa Monica built, C-53D Skytrooper transport, built in March 1942, which after military service went to TWA in May 1945 as a DC-3A and in November 1949 with over 18,000 hours on the airframe was declared surplus with the airline. After three private owners it was purchased by Conroy Inc. at Santa Barbara, California who fitted it with two Rolls-Royce Dart turboprops taken from a United Air Lines Viscount aircraft. Known as *The Turbo Three* it first flew on May 13, 1969.

Eight years later the aircraft appeared with Specialised Aircraft Corporation fitted with three Pratt & Whitney PT-6 turboprops and named *Spirit of Hope*. During 1979 it was carrying Polair livery, fitted with skis and on lease to the US Navy in Alaska. A year later it was seen in storage at its home base at Camarillo, Oxnard, California. This photograph was taken when the aircraft was included in the 1978 Farnborough Air Show. A military version involving Super DC-3 airframes including a swing-tail fuselage never materialised.

Bonanza Air Lines of Las Vegas commenced inter-state service on August 5, 1946, being founded on the last day of 1945. Certificated on June 15, 1949, with the first DC-3 service on December 19 on the route Reno - Las Vegas - Phoenix, with a later extension to Los Angeles. The Las Vegas - Phoenix route was transferred from TWA. This Bonanza DC-3 N491 was a model DC-3A-269B built during 1940 for Northwest. In June 1942 it was impressed into military service as a C-48B with the USAAF, returning to Northwest in July 1944. It was sold to Bonanza in May 1955 after which it served overseas with airlines in Japan and Korea.

Douglas AC-47 Gunship from the 4th Special Operations Squadron, 14th Special Operations Wing, on patrol over Vietnam airspace, one of many C-47s converted for use in the South East Asia conflict by the USAF. Pilots declared the AC-47 an extraordinary simple aircraft to operate, for in all other aspects except the armament, she was just an overloaded DC-3 or C-47, with very similar flight characteristics.

Some disadvantages were that crews were flying a transport usually years older than themselves, they having little or no flight time in propeller aircraft, and being always over gross weight the transport was tail heavy. In addition to the mini-gun installation, the forward cargo hold was modified to carry 24,000 rounds of 7.62 mm ammunition and forty-five 200,000 candlepower flares, which could be tossed out of the open cargo hatch. During 1969 the AC-47 Gunship was phased out in favour of larger aircraft such as the AC-119 Flying Boxcar, and the AC-130 Hercules gunships.

The close-up shows the gun positions on the AC-47. Each mini-gun was capable of firing either 3,000 or 6,000 rounds per minute. With all three guns firing at the same time, which was rarely done, an AC-47 could put down 18,000 rounds per minute. It was an awesome sight.

Seen at Van Nuys Airport, California, on November 10, 1968, is yet another DC-3 retaining its original 'N' number. Manufactured at Santa Monica in August 1941 it was one of a large fleet ordered for Hawaiian Airlines. It was converted by them to Viewmaster configuration, with panoramic viewing windows during 1955, returning to California to serve with various local airlines well into the 1960s. It is portrayed here in the livery of Quickie Vacations Ltd. of Phoenix, Arizona, so was evidently visiting Van Nuys. In January 1969 it was sold to Holiday Aircraft Sales & Leasing and re-registered N8720. Sometime after 1975 it was cancelled from the US Civil Register.

At the beginning of World War 2, there were three established airlines in India. As the war progressed scheduled services disappeared in favour of contract work in a semi-military role. On March 1, 1944, Tata Air Lines introduced Douglas DC-3s and just over a year later were allocated four war-surplus C-47s and bought and leased eight others direct from the US Foreign Liquidation Commission. On July 29, 1946 its name was changed to Air India.

Indian National Airways based at New Delhi, operated a number of wartime routes, mainly to Madras, Bombay and Karachi. Douglas DC-2s entered service in October 1942. At the end of World War 2 six DC-3s were purchased. Air Services of India operated a fleet of eleven DC-3s covering Lucknow, Karachi, Bagalore and Cochin. Deccan Airways founded on September 21, 1945, commenced service on July 1, 1946, with a fleet of a dozen DC-3s. Three other airlines, all with fleets of DC-3s made minor postwar contributions.

On August 1, 1953, eight former independent companies became 'lines' of the Indian Airline Corporation operating a total of 74 DC-3s. These Douglas transports remained to provide the backbone of the feeder services for many years. In fact the greater part of the 74 aircraft were still giving excellent service in the late 1960s. Shown is VT-DDD, an ex-RAF Dakota KG717 built at Oklahoma City in 1942. Today the Indian Air Force is planning to replace its 40 odd Douglas C-47 transports with a more modern type.

This unique Douglas DC-3, seen at Miami during 1970, is surely the world's most political flying billboard. The aircraft is a veteran and is believed to be still in service in the USA. It was completed at Santa Monica during October 1942 for Trans Continental & Western Air — TWA — but not taken up as it was impressed into USAAF service as a Douglas C-49, serving from 1942 until June 1945. It then went to TWA remaining with this airline until May 1950. It became registered N230D during 1966 and it is believed it was owned by one Chuck Hall of Miami when this photograph was taken during 1970.

Spectacular line-up of a dozen surplus BOAC Dakotas at London Airport during March 1949, awaiting disposal. The first in line G-AGKF was purchased by the airline on September 9, 1944, and loaned to British European Airways in 1946, before purchase by Field Aircraft Services in June 1949. It crashed in Africa in January the following year. The second, G-AGNF, was also purchased by Field Aircraft Services, and sold to the Union of Burma Airways.

By the end of hostilities BOAC had accepted fifty-nine Dakotas, delivery of the majority being by way of the North Atlantic ferry route under No. 45 Group in Canada. Most went direct to BOAC but others spent short periods with RAF units beforehand.

Rare photograph taken at Mascot Airport, Essendon, Australia during December 1969, of DC-3C VH-AEQ, used to celebrate the 50th Anniversary of Air Mail between England, Singapore and Australia. The aircraft also carries adverts for Mildara wines, John Mack cameras, Shell refuelling and Kings tours.

This Douglas transport was built at Long Beach as a C-47 Skytrain in March 1942, serving with the US 5th Air Force in Australia and named *Aeolus*. It survived World War 2, had a series of owners and was badly damaged at Mascot on November 4, 1957, but was repaired and finally retired in 1973, being still derelict at Brisbane in 1977. Latest reports indicate that the aircraft is preserved at Chewing Gum Field Museum, Tallebudgera, Queensland.

Various Douglas DC-2 and DC-3 transports were captured by German invading forces in Czechoslovakia, Poland, and finally in the Netherlands between 1938 and 1940. Some of these were impressed as military transports by the Luftwaffe, others went to Lufthansa. When the post-war Luftwaffe was reformed in 1956, a number of ex-RAF Dakotas were refurbished under a reverse Lend-Lease agreement with the USAF who bore the cost. They were test flown in USAF livery in the United Kingdom. Over 50 Daks were involved of which 20 went to the Luftwaffe serving with many units.

The C-47 in the photograph which belongs to Transport Geschwader 61 based at Neubiberg, was originally delivered to the RAF as KN597 on May 10, 1945, and a month later was serving in Air Command South-East Asia — ACSEA — before storage with No. 22 Maintenance Unit at Silloth in Cumberland. It was selected for refurbishing in April 1955, and took nearly a year to rebuild, becoming 44-76906 in February 1956 with delivery to the USAF-operated 7330th Pilot Training Group at Furstenfeldbruck. Today this C-47 is with Air Cargo America in Miami, Florida.

The Uganda Air Force was formed from the Police Air Wing during 1964/65, remaining under Army control, and obtained its first combat aircraft in 1966. With the help of West Germany, Czechoslovakia, Israel and Libya, it was gradually developed. During the Amin regime it never attained a very credible operational status, despite the efforts of a Soviet air mission plus the ambitious plans of Idi Amin himself. Since the change of government in 1979 there appears to have been very little significant improvement. At least 6 Douglas C-47 transports are in service, most possibly ex-Israeli Defence Force aircraft and based at Entebbe with a transport unit of assorted aircraft and helicopters.

Sources and numbers of Douglas C-47 military transports currently in service with the Zimbabwe, formerly Rhodesian, Air Force, are difficult to assess. Many are camouflaged and often do not carry the national insignia or serial numbers. Transport tasks are allocated to No. 3 Squadron based at the main air base of New Sarum, attached to Salisbury airport. These C-47s contributed to the 'Fire Force' which provided transports for paratroop operations into neighbouring Zambian territory in 'search and destroy' missions. The photograph shows a camouflaged No. 3 Squadron Dakota with paratroops resting in the foreground.

Hunting Aerosurveys Ltd. and Hunting Geophysics Ltd., operated this interesting DC-3 conversion during the 1950/60s. The sting in the tail houses the magnetometer head, whilst the 'bird' towed below the aircraft carries the electromagnetic detector head. The cradle in which the 'bird' is housed for take-off and landing is visible below the fuselage.

Also visible is the horizontal transmitting coil for the electromagnetometer; this is carried from the belly of the fuselage to anchorages on the main plane, thence via fuselage outriggers to the tail plane, and from there below the fuselage just ahead of the tail wheel to a similar array on the other side. The array on top of the fuselage carries a compensating coil to counteract the effect of the aircraft on the responses of the instrument.

The Dakota could also be fitted out as a photographic survey aircraft and in this role completed an extensive tour in South West Africa, Kenya, Somalia and Libya during 1960. The fitting of two Pratt & Whitney 1830/90C 2-speed Twin Wasp engines increased the ceiling to 28,000 feet and in those days it was probably one of the most advanced survey aircraft in civil employment.

The wartime US Naval Air Transport Service — NATS — operated twelve squadrons of Douglas transports, including the Douglas R4D prior to being merged with the huge Military Air Transport Service — MATS — towards the end of World War 2. When the Mid Atlantic Air Museum located at Harrisburg International Airport purchased a surplus US Navy R4D-6 in November 1980, it was decided to restore it to its original NATS configuration.

Manufactured in 1944 at the Oklahoma City factory, it operated with VR-2 Squadron at NAS Norfolk, Virginia. It was declared surplus in 1959 and stored at Litchfield Park, Arizona, and later operated with the FAA who used a fleet of no less than 20 Douglas R4D transports for flight checking radar. From 1978 the US Forest Service used the transport for two years.

The wonderful authentic restoration was virtually done by volunteers, all members, male and female, of the museum. Their hard work has not been in vain, for in 1982 the large Navy transport won the Best Transport Award at Oshkosh, and in 1983 the ultimate — the Grand Champion Award.

Bordering on what was once British Honduras, now Belize, Guatemala is the most northerly of the Republic States of Central America, becoming a signatory to the Rio Pact of Mutual Defence in 1947. During World War 2 the USA granted cash credits to Guatemala under the Lease-Lend Act for the purchase of defence materials, in return for facilities to build defence bases. Small numbers of Douglas C-47 transports were included in the aircraft provided. In 1945 a USAF Mission arrived to reorganise the country's military aviation, and today a number of C-47s still remain in service. To counter an escalating guerilla activity in the country, US assistance has been resumed. The C-47s are now finished in the latest low-visibility markings, overall green or brown finish, and are employed on anti-guerilla operations. This photograph shows C-47 '540' which visited Kelly AFB in Texas on November 4, 1972, and is still believed to be in service.

This Douglas DC-3 transport, N133D, currently operated by Academy Airlines of Griffin, Georgia, was the sixth DST built, being delivered to American Airlines on July 12, 1936. Today it is the oldest surviving DC-3. This venerable transport holds the honour of being the oldest type of aircraft ever to use the shuttle landing facility at the NASA Kennedy Space Center in Florida. It airlifted the auxiliary power units for Orbiter Challenger back to the manufacturer for overhaul. During World War 2, as a USAAF C-49E, the transport flew with the North Atlantic Wing of Air Transport Command and today the total time flown since leaving the Santa Monica factory exceeds 72,000 hours, roughly the equivalent of 8.2 years of non-stop, around the clock operation.

The first of an initial batch of 58 Dakotas for the South African Air Force arrived in the country during June 1943, being Lend-Lease aircraft from RAF orders delivered direct from the Douglas factories. The very first SAAF Dakota '6801' ex-RAF FD874, is today still very active with No. 3 Squadron of the Zimbabwe Air Force.

When No. 28 Squadron returned to South Africa after World War 2 service in October 1945, it took 26 RAF Dakotas with it, these being transferred to the SAAF. South Africa was one of the three Commonwealth countries who supplied Dakota crews for the Berlin Airlift in 1948. Today, after 45 years of excellent service, the Dakota is still a front-line type with an estimated 50 on inventory. This superb photograph of '6868' was taken during late 1984. It was originally a Lend-Lease C-47 for the Royal New Zealand Air Force delivered in May 1945, and purchased by the SAAF in January 1981.

During 1979 this was possibly the only Douglas DC-3 roaming the highways of Southern California. Smokey Rowlands of Cardiff-on-Sea, south of the Douglas factory at Long Beach, purchased the aircraft from the graveyard at Davis Monthan Air Force Base, Tucson, Arizona and removed the wings, engines and tail assembly. The fuselage had to be cut at the rear by four feet to comply with road regulations. The fuselage is mounted on a former Dodge school bus chassis, and the power is from a 7-litre Lincoln Continental engine giving 10 miles per gallon. The fuselage has two 65-gallon tanks and the owner claimed he could cruise 1,300 miles without a pit stop. The DC-3 is reputed to have flown 10 years with Argonaut Airlines in Florida before going to Allegheny Airlines. According to the records she had been hijacked twice to Cuba.

On September 11, 1939, four Douglas DC-3s were chartered from Australian National Airways and impressed for Royal Australian Air Force transport duties. These aircraft operated for a limited period and by mid-1940 had been returned to Australian National Airways. Dakotas began operating with the RAAF in February 1943 and deliveries included nine Dakota Mk. Is, fifty Dakota Mk. IIIs and sixty-five Dakota Mk. IVs. In addition the RAAF operated twenty-three C-53 Skytroopers and one impressed C-49 on loan from the USAAF. Post-war the Dakota has served wherever the RAAF has operated.

By mid-1962 it was estimated that these Daks had flown in excess of half-a-million hours in RAAF service. Today five C-47 Dakota transports still serve the RAAF, to be phased out as 1990 approaches, and all serve with the Aircraft Research and Development Unit — ARDU — based at Edinburgh Field, New South Wales. On February 13, 1984, all five Daks were launched, possibly the very last RAAF five aircraft formation and this close-up of A65-95 was taken during this flight some 45 miles north of Adelaide.

This immaculate DC-3 belongs to Wiley Sanders, a collector of vintage
aircraft. It was built at Long Beach in May 1942 as C-47-DL, stayed in the
USA during World War 2 operated by Braniff crews, and, in March 1946
became NC13719 with Air Cargo Transport. Since then it has served several
owners, the last one recorded with the author, being the Long Beach
Development Corporation during 1979. It was first registered N728G — its
registration today — in October 1969 when the aircraft was owned and
operated by the Republic National Bank of Dallas.

Delivered to Eastern Air Lines on December 7, 1937, the last passenger flight of DC-3, N18124, took place on October 12, 1952. The veteran had completed nearly 57,000 hours in the air, equivalent to 6½ years flying non-stop. Captain Eddie Rickenbacker, President of the Airline, presented the transport to the Smithsonian Institute on May 1, 1953. Photographs shows the DC-3 being renovated by Eastern Air Lines personnel ready for permanent display in the National Air and Space Museum — NASM — in Washington which opened on July 1, 1976. It is now on show alongside other transport veterans.

Suidwes Lugdiens (Edms) Bepark of Windhoek, South West Africa, today known as Namibia, originated as South West Air Transport Limited until it merged with Oryx Aviation in March 1959. The first DC-3 was purchased in November 1953, and two remained in 1978 when Namib Air was formed. Photograph shows a modern day jeep being prepared for loading into Dakota ZS-DIW. This is an early RAF Dakota delivered to the Middle East in December 1943 and after use by No. 28 Squadron South African Air Force returned home with the Squadron in October 1945. It was civilianised in November 1953 and as far as is known is still today serving with Namib Air.

On the first day of October 1950 the Royal Danish Air Force was formed. Being a founder member of NATO the RDAF received assistance from the USA under the Military Defence Aid Programme — MDAP — with not only aircraft, but the rebuilding of seven airfields, plus a control and reporting radar system.

During September 1953, a Douglas C-47 transport flight was formed within Eskadrille 721, initially being equipped with two DC-3 transports ex-Scandinavian Airlines. Three years later this flight was considerably strengthened when the USAF transferred six C-47s formerly used by the Royal Norwegian Air Force. These transports were based at Vaerlose, two being retired in 1981, the remainder disposed of only recently in the United Kingdom and in the USA. During 1953 the C-47s took part, in paratroop training with the Joegerkorpset (Hunter Corps.), a Ranger unit under Army control, south of Aalborg.

SATENA — Servicio de Aeronavegacion a Territorios Nacionales — is unique in that it is part of the Military Air Transport Command of the Colombian Air Force. However its aircraft, including C-47s are used on regular airline internal routes, and on paramilitary duties as required. SATENA was formed in April 1961 and it is amongst the major users of the C-47 in South America.

As the transport became surplus to requirements with the USAF, so further aircraft were supplied to Colombia from the huge storage depot located at Davis-Monthan in Arizona. This C-47 FAC-1126 was photographed at San Andres Island, Colombia on June 29, 1980. After delivery to the USAF in July 1945 it served with Strategic Air Command, and after storage was delivered to SATENA in April 1976.

QANTAS Empire Airways Ltd. operated C-47s in the latter part of World War 2 on loan from the USAF and subsequently converted a fleet of DC-3s for passenger work in Australia and New Guinea, commencing service in 1946. This immaculate DC-3 VH-EDD is unique in that it was delivered as a C-47 in July 1944, serving with No. 33 Squadron RAAF during the war. After a period of civilian use it went to the Royal Netherlands Air Force in August 1962 becoming VH-EDD in January 1964 with QANTAS, one of a fleet of 18 similar transports. It was sold to the Queensland Pacific Trading Company in December 1971.

Today, in 1985, the many airports and airstrips around Miami, Florida are a haven for the Douglas DC-3. At Miami International Airport, the twelve strong fleet of immaculate DC-3 transports of PBA — Provincetown Boston Airline — based at Naples, Florida, mingle well with the modern jet liners as they carry commuters on a hub and spoke system connecting the backwoods with the main air terminals. It is said that many DC-3s have been so heavily modified over the years, that the only item remaining that is original is the serial number. This can be said of N84KB with its VIP interior including window curtains, panoramic windows, modified engines, undercarriage and wings, plus air stair. It is one of two such DC-3s owned by the Context Realty Development Corporation who operate these for flights to the company's land holdings and real estate developments in Florida.

N84KB is a 1943 US Navy R4D-1 transport civilianised in 1946. The photograph of the two DC-3s parked is unique in that both were on the pre-war Santa Monica production line together in 1940 — N21797 c/n 2201 delivered on March 4 and N34PB c/n 2204 on March 12, both to American Airlines. Over 40 years later they are seen together again, both in immaculate condition, both retaining the starboard single passenger door, now with air stair, and both operated by PBA, the largest commuter airline in the USA.

This Douglas DC-3 is mounted on a single, rotating pedestal which allows the aircraft to weathercock into the wind, like a weathervane. The DC-3, that once flew along the Yukon, British Columbia and Alberta routes for Canadian Pacific, is today a monument at Whitehorse Airport, Yukon. Restoration of the aeroplane, first registered to CPA in 1946, was undertaken by the Yukon Flying Club in 1977. The aircraft had sat derelict at the south end of Whitehorse Airport since 1970, abandoned after blowing an engine on an attempted take-off.

Photographic Acknowledgements

Douglas Aircraft Company, 3855 Lakewood Boulevard, LONG BEACH, California 90846, USA.
Page 7, 9, 11, 12, 13, 16, 17, 18, 22, 30, 35, 36, 41, 48 bottom, 52 bottom, 55, 58 bottom, 59, 61, 62, 63, 64, 66, 68, 69, 70, 71, 76, 81, 131.

Arthur Pearcy, AP Publications, The Flat, Royden House, Odell Road, SHARNBROOK, Beds., England.
33, 34, 51, 53, 78 top, 82, 89, 98 top, 107, 108, 110, 122, 129, 130, 132, 134, 136, 137, 143, 144, 151, 158, 162.

William T. Larkins, 175 Clarie Drive, PLEASANT HILL, California 94523, USA.
15, 25, 26, 92, top/bottom, 97, 160.

Peter M. Bowers, 10458 16th Avenue South, SEATTLE, Washington 98168, USA.
37 top/bottom, 45, 50, 60, top/bottom, 142 top.

Peter R. Keating, 3 Edinburgh Close, ICKENHAM, Middlesex UB10 8RA, England.
90, 98 top/bottom, 124, 146, 148, 152.

Imperial War Museum, Lambeth Road, London SE1 6HE, England.
43, 44, 49, 52 top, 57, 78 bottom, 80.

Norman Taylor, 114 Wildwood Drive, FLORENCE, South Carolina 29501, USA.
67, 75, 105, 121, 145 top, 156.

Lee C. Bright, Eastern Air Lines, International Airport, MIAMI, Florida 33148, USA.
38, 87, 161 top, 165 top/bottom.

Louis J. Vosloo, 35 Echo Road, PO Box 55, 7975 FISH HOEK, Republic of South Africa.
113, 114, 139, 157.

Stephen Piercy Collection, c/o Arthur Pearcy.
56, 93, 147, 156 bottom.

American Airlines, PO Box 61616, DALLAS/FORT WORTH AIRPORT, Texas 75261, USA.
8, 14, 23, 31.

US Naval Historical Centre, Washington Navy Yard, Building 57, WASHINGTON DC 20374, USA.
73, 103, 104, 117.

Gordon S. Williams, 2023 92nd Avenue NE., Clyde Hill, BELLEVUE, Washington 98004, USA.
7 top, 28, 166.

United Nations, 20 Buckingham Gate, LONDON W1E 6LB, England.
126, 127, 141.

KLM — Dutch Royal Airlines, 55 Amsterdamseweg, AMSTELVEEN, The Netherlands
19, 32, 79.

USAF — Office of Public Affairs, 1221 South Fern Street, Room D-159, ARLINGTON, Virginia 22202, USA.
46, 83, 125.

British Airways, Speedbird House, London (Heathrow) Airport, HOUNSLOW, Middlesex, England.
72 bottom, 99, 100.

Ministry of Defence (Air), Room 69, Fourth Floor, King Charles Street, LONDON SW.1, England.
84, 85, 115.

National Archives, General Service Adminstration, WASHINGTON DC 20405, USA.
65, 101, 102.

Michael O'Leary, Challenge Publications, 7950 Deering Avenue, CANOGA PARK, California 91304, USA.
95, 135.

Quadrant Picture Library, Quadrant House, The Quadrant, SUTTON, Surrey SM2 5AS, England.
112, 149.

Canadian Armed Forces (Air), Information Service, Dept of National Defence, MDHQ. OTTAWA, Ontario K1A 0K2, Canada.
72 top, 91.

Australian War Memorial, CANBERRA ACT, Australia.
42, 47.

United Air Lines, PO Box 66100, CHICAGO, Illinois 60666, USA.
10, 27.

Field Aircraft Services Ltd., No.2 Maintenance Area, London (Heathrow) Airport, HOUNSLOW, Middlesex, England.
118 top/bottom.

Ferranti Limited, HOLLINWOOD, Lancashire OL9 7JS, England.
128 top/bottom.

Kirby Harrison, c/o Naval Aviation News, Building 159E, Room 590, Washington Navy Yard Annexe, WASHINGTON DC 20374, USA.
155 top/bottom.

Rev. Boardman C. Reed, PO Box 337, Aero Pines, BROWNSVILLE, California 95919, USA.
54.

Kent Kistler, 3506 221st Avenue SE., ISSAQUAH, Washington 98027, USA.
88.

Roger Wright, 8 Ettingham Close, WELLESBOURNE, Warwickshire CV35 9RJ, England.
140.

Norman Thelwell, 10 Graydon Avenue, CHICHESTER, West Sussex PO19 2RF, England.
163.

RNZAF, Central Photo Establishment, RNZAF Base OHAKEA, New Zealand.
120.

TIME/LIFE, Rockefeller Center, NEW YORK, New York 10020, USA.
48 top.

National Air & Space Museum, Smithsonian Institution, WASHINGTON DC 20560, USA.
161 bottom.

TWA — .Trans World Airlines, 605 Third Avenue, NEW YORK, NY 10158, USA.
24.

Robert C. Mikesh, 5201 Oahu Court, CAMP SPRINGS, Maryland 20031, USA.
145.

Hawaiian Airlines, PO Box 30008, HONOLULU INTL. AIRPORT, Honolulu, Hawaii 96820, USA.
29.

Delta Air Lines, Hartsfield Atlanta Intl. Airport, ATLANTA, Georgia 30320, USA.
40 bottom.

Braniff Airways, 7701 Lemon Avenue, DALLAS, Texas 75209, USA.
39 top.

Air France, 1 Square Max Hymons, 75757 PARIS CEDEX 15, France.
119.

Scottish Aviation, Prestwick Airport, PRESTWICK, Ayrshire KA9 2PL, Scotland.
106.

Turkish Air Force, Press & Public Relations, MoD., Milli Savunma Pakanligi, Bakanlilar, ANKARA, Turkey.
116.

Western Air Lines, 6060 Avion Drive, LOS ANGELES, California 90045, USA.
111.

Chief Pilot Tim Sarginson, Sunbird Aviation Ltd., PO Box 4627, NAIROBI, Kenya.
138.

QANTAS Airways, Qantas Intl. Centre, PO Box 489, SYDNEY, NSW., Australia.
164.

Danish Air Force, Public Information Office, PO 202, DK-2950 VEDBAEK, Denmark.
162.

Director du Service d'Information et des Relations Publiques des Armées, Ministre de la Défense Nationale, Boulevard St.-Germain, PARIS, France.
142 bottom.

Martin J. Willing, Cathay Pacific Airways, Swire House, 9 Connaught Road, C, HONG KONG.
96

Mrs. Pat Dufeu, 9 Thorncroft, HORNCHURCH, Essex RM11 1EU, England.
58 top.

Director of Army Aviation, ACSFOR, Dept. of the US Army, The Pentagon, WASHINGTON DC 20310, USA.
74.

Armstrong Siddeley.
100 bottom.

Merle Olmstead, California, USA.
86

James Muncie
123

Hunting Aero Surveys, Elstree Way, BOREHAMWOOD, Herts., England.
154.

US Aircraft Corporation, Burbank Airport, BURBANK, California 91520, USA.
133.

Photographers International
153.

Dutch Dakota Association, Postbus 75090, 1117 ZP SCHIPHOL, The Netherlands.
94.

N.Z.N.A.C., Air New Zealand House, 1 Queen Street, AUCKLAND, New Zealand.
109.

RAAF, Air Research & Development Unit, ARDU., Edinburgh Field, South Australia.
160.

Austin J. Brown, LBIPP., 3 Berkeley Crescent, Clifton, BRISTOL BS8 1HA, England.
Front and rear book jacket photo.